CHANGING THE TIDE

LESSONS IN HORSEMANSHIP

CHANGING THE TIDE

LESSONS IN HORSEMANSHIP

ROSS JACOBS

Copyright © 2012 by Ross Jacobs

The right of Ross Jacobs to be identified as the author of this work has been asserted by him in accordance with the Copyright, Designs and Patents Act 1988.

This edition published in 2012 by Ross Jacobs

ISBN: 978-0-646-59043-1

All rights reserved. Without limiting the rights under copyright reserved above, this publication may not be reproduced, stored or transmitted by any means, without prior permission of the copyright holder/publisher.

This book is a work of fiction. Any resemblance to actual persons, living or dead, events or locales is entirely coincidental.

Typesetting by Wordzworth.com

www.goodhorsemanship.com.au

This book is dedicated to the love of my life, Michèle.

CONTENTS

ACKNOWLEDGEMENTS	iii
PREFACE	v
MENTORING	1
THE CRANKY HORSE	5
THE NOT SO SIMPLE ART OF HORSE TRAINING	11
THE ONE REIN STOP	15
BARRY AND CEDAR	21
IT FELT RIGHT AT THE TIME	27
WALT AND THE FOAL	33
NONE OF YOUR BEESWAX	37
THE ROUTINE OF CHANGE	43
FERRET GRASS	47
IT'S NOT EASY BEING GREEN	51
MOTIVATION TO SEARCH	57
WHAT IS A TRICK?	61
CAN A HORSE ENJOY WORK?	65
FOOD, GLORIOUS FOOD	71
STRAIGHT AS A VICAR IN A COFFIN	75

TRAINING MOZ	81
CHASING A REACTION	91
CHARLIE	99
THE PLIGHT OF ENRICO	105
PICKINESS	109
RUSTY AND ME	117
A HORSE'S LIMITATIONS ARE OUR LIMITATIONS	123
THE ART OF COMMUNICATION	133
FEEDING TIME	137
THE ROUND YARD	143
THE WORLD IS A BOX	149
OLD DRESSAGE VERSUS NEW DRESSAGE	155
TRAINING WITH INTENT	161
TRAINING AND CHOICES	165
WHY IS IT SO?	171

ACKNOWLEDGEMENTS

All of the stories in this work have appeared at one time or another in the magazine, Chaff Chat. I want to thank the editor, Des Miller for her continuing support and friendship.

My appreciation goes out to Harry Whitney, who has remained a close friend and who provided the inspiration for some of the stories. My many thanks to Tom Moates, who provided the incentive to write the first book and was constantly encouraging me to compile the present volume.

Most important of all goes my love and gratitude to Michèle, my wife. In a practical sense she acted as a critic, editor and cover designer. But more than that she is the best thing in my life. The constant I can count on at all times and through all things.

Finally I have to give credit and thanks to all the people and horses with whom I have crossed paths. The one thing that books, dvds and talk cannot replace is experience. Without the opportunity to work with the huge number of people and horses that has been my good fortune, the concepts presented in the stories would be empty and meaningless. Nobody becomes a good horse person without a lot of experience and I cannot express my appreciation enough for those that gave that to me.

PREFACE

This book is the second volume of a collection of stories written for Chaff Chat, a magazine published each month by the Horse Riders Clubs Association of Victoria. They are in no order and follow no logical or chronological sequence. Each stands on it's own.

The stories present concepts and a philosophical approach to working with horses that has been practiced by good horse people for a very long time. There are very few references to actual training techniques in the book. The purpose of the stories is not to teach people how to train horses. Rather, they are written to help people discover a way of approaching the training process.

I feel that as time passes many people have less time to devote to their horses and horsemanship. Time is allocated into getting the training done as quickly as possible because there is little room for anything else. This leads to shortcuts and tricks in training and a lack of deep appreciation of the amazing animal in our lives. More people are interested in how to make a horse do something and less interested in how to encourage a horse to want to do something. This is not the message that Walt and Amos try to pass on to the young boy in the stories.

In the story titled Charlie, Walt makes the observation that most people try to make their horse be something that it want it to be. But very few people try to be the person their horse needs them to be. This book is a very small attempt to redress that balance.

Ross Jacobs

MENTORING

"Do you ever get sick and tired of all my questions, Walt?" I asked. I had been having particular difficulty with a foal I had been handling for Mrs Farley. The foal was one tough filly who it seemed would rather kick me in the head than eat or breathe. She was only about 3 weeks old, but already didn't care when her mum would wander off or if the other foals were around. It was savage when it attacked mum for a feed and just overall seemed angry at the world. The other foals would play and cavort like foals do, but this filly didn't play. Whenever she interacted with the other foals it was war. There was no play. It was not about fun, it was battle!

I remember the first time I got a halter on her. Without any pressure from the lead rope the foal threw herself to the ground. There was no pulling back and loss of balance. There was no rear and a stumble. She just collapsed like all four legs snapped in two. When she got up, she did it again and then again and again. I had never seen a horse do that before. I was terrified she was going to hurt herself, but she seemed to know what she was doing and had rehearsed it to perfection like a stunt for a movie. I found it very unnerving and was desperate for help from Walt. I got the halter off her as soon as possible and ran to find the old man.

I told Walt what had happened.

"Mmm, matey. Sounds like ya grabbed the tail of a big ol' croc. Ya lucky ya didn't get eaten alive."

"But what do I do about it, Walt? This filly is crazy. She is either going to kill me or I'm going to kill her. I think I need your help. I don't know what to do."

"Well I'm busy now matey. Put her away and I'll look at her tomorrow for ya. Old Bev Farley won't mind waitin another day and neither will that croc."

It didn't escape my notice that Walt referred to Mrs Farley as "old" despite her being several years his junior.

The following day I led the mare into the stockyard and the filly followed with a bit of help from Mrs Farley driving her from behind. I put the mare on one side of the yards to separate her from the filly while we waited for Walt.

Soon enough I heard an uneven crunching on the gravel path and knew that Walt's bandy legs were dragging him our way. He had a long rope and a stick in his hands.

"Okay matey, why don't ya go and catch the little angel and let me see what we see."

I managed to corner her in the yard closest to her mum and ran my hand along her rump and over her back. It took no time before I was able to stroke her neck and face. She didn't react to my hand, but she gave me a look that said I had better sleep with one eye open for a while. It was only a few moments later that I was able to get the head collar on her. I didn't pull on the lead rope at all, but clucked with my tongue to get her to move out of the corner. It was enough to send her flying to the other end of the yard where she turned and gave me that same look. It was a look that said "I know where you live and I know where your family live."

I stepped to my left about three paces and slowly took up the slack in the lead rope. Even before the rope became taut Satan's child shook her head violently then threw herself down so she was lying on her left side. She then got half way up and threw herself down again. Then she thrashed for two or three seconds before getting a third of the way up and throwing herself down again. I got scared and as I was about to turn to Walt for help when I felt him beside me. He grabbed the lead rope from me at the same time saying, "Step back, matey." The filly kept rising part way and then throwing herself down again. I saw Walt swing the tail end of the rope and begin to beat the ground with extreme violence – missing the foal by only a couple of feet. The filly leapt to her feet and looked at Walt. It was a perplexed look, like she was trying to figure out what had happened.

A few seconds passed when the foal began to shake her head, preparing to throw herself to the ground again. This time Walt whacked the ground hard enough for it to register as an earth tremor in another continent. The filly jumped to the side, stopped shaking and looked at Walt again. This happened another three times and each time Walt interrupted her by whacking the ground.

At this point Walt stepped to the side and put enough feel on the lead rope to take the slack out it. Soon the filly began to fling her head to which Walt responded by blowing a raspberry and stamping his feet like it was grape crushing season in Tuscany, and at the same time keeping the feel on the rope. He had to repeat this twice more and then the filly stepped her hindquarters around so she was facing him, but with head shaking. This exercise was done again and again until the filly would step around to keep facing Walt wherever he walked, without any shenanigans or pulling against the lead rope. From this point it didn't take long before the foal was stepping forward from a feel on the lead rope. She had given up her tantrums for that day.

We finished the session at that point and Mrs Farley was very pleased. On the other hand I felt more confused and inadequate than pleased. I barraged Walt with questions which he answered in his often non-answer way. Just when Walt felt he had given me the secret to foal training that only truly great zen foal trainers understood, I had one last question. There was so many things I didn't understand I knew I couldn't wait to be as old as Walt before I understood them – it was just too long to wait.

"Do you ever get sick and tired of all my questions, Walt?"

"Yeah matey, sometimes."

"I'm sorry, I don't mean to be a nuisance," I said.

"Matey, when I was a young fella – not much older than ya self - I worked on a stock camp in Queensland. Every season we were given six horses for the muster. Them horses were pretty wild. They'd run feral most of the year and be brought into camp to be ridden for four weeks of musterin. Then after musterin was over they'd be put out in a fifty thousand acre paddock again for another six months. When we'd round 'em up to get 'em ready for the muster they wouldn't let ya touch 'em. And when ya got a saddle on 'em they'd buck and kick a hole in the sky.

"One year there was a bloke who came to work for the boss who seem to have a lot less trouble than the rest of us fools. He was real quiet around people and horses and seemed to get along with just about any horse he was given. Fact is he was given the worst of 'em because the boss knew he could get somethin done with 'em. I watched him turn one horse that was known to run off on ya every ride into the best cow horse on the place. But nobody seemed too interested in what this fella was doin different to get the best out them horses. They just wanted him to get the horses goin good and how he did it wasn't real important to anybody. Well, anybody but me and Amos.

"We took some time to watch him whenever he put a horse in the yard. We was young and shy and didn't want to bother him with lots of stupid questions. Besides the other blokes would think we was slackin if we spent too much time watchin and talkin. But the fella noticed us watchin him a lot and one day came over to talk to us about the horse he was workin. He was a pretty friendly bloke. We got into discussin horses and what made 'em tick.

"At one point I said to him I was sorry for askin so many questions and botherin him so much."

"Son, why would it be any botha? I don't mind a bit. Ya know, I love these animals and anythin that I can do that can make their life better I'm happy to do. That includes helpin people who want my help because some day that's gonna help another horse. Those other nongs don't care and they would just be wastin my time, but you blokes love the horses as much as I do. Helpin you fellas be better horse handlers is doin somethin for the horses. Who knows one day ya'll probably be betta than me and you'll help some kid leanin over the fence of your yard wantin to know more.

"Matey, I have never forgotten what he said to Amos and me. And I say the same to you. Why would it botha me to answer ya questions if it will help a horse? You love them horses as much as I do. One day you'll probably be betta than me and you'll be able to help some kid leanin over the fence of your yard wantin to know more."

THE CRANKY HORSE

I had only just arrived at the riding school to begin work for the day. It was a beautiful autumn Sydney day and I was really looking forward to having a lesson with Amos on his horse, Calico. As I walked up the driveway towards the main house I saw a crowd making way for a car coming out for the gateway to the stable block. It all looked a bit strange and I sensed something was wrong.

The car was coming towards me and accelerating as it made its way out to the road. As it passed I saw Mr Fox driving and Mrs Fox with her arms around her daughter Zoe as if cradling her.

One of the regular girls that hung around the riding school all weekend was Penny.

"Hey Pen. Is Zoe okay? What's going on?" I asked.

"Piper bit her. She got her right on the arm and it is really deep. I've never seen so much blood!"

"Well what happened?" I asked again.

"I think Zoe was saddling her up for a lesson with Tony and as she did the girth tighter Piper reached around and got her on the arm, just above the wrist. Boy, did she yell. Zoe gave her a whack on the face and didn't even realize how bad the bite was for a minute until she saw the blood soaking through her jumper. Mr Fox thinks she might have broken her arm. Anyway, they're taking her to the hospital."

"I hope she'll be okay," I said.

I knew Penny and Zoe were part of the same group, so I'd hear all the latest gossip on Zoe from her.

Sure enough, the next day Penny came up to me and told me that Piper's bite did break a bone in Zoe's wrist and she would have it in a cast for about 6 weeks.

The next weekend, the boss found me watching Amos and Walt start a new filly they bought from the auction.

"I got a call from Zoe's mum yesterday. She said they need somebody to keep Piper in work until Zoe is right enough to get back to riding. She asked me if I knew anybody. They'll pay $5 a ride. Do you want to do it?"

I thought for a minute if I really needed the money versus just how dangerous a biter is Piper.

"Sure. I can ride the horse a few days each week."

The next day I decided I should at least make my introductions to Piper. I went to see her in the paddock. She watched me coming and seem to be okay about it. She didn't move or swish her tail. But as I got within a metre of her head she looked away and flattened her ears. I gently stroked her on the neck and her ears relaxed. Scratching her under the neck seemed to be the thing that made the most difference. She stretched her neck high and twisted her head to the side as her top lip protruded way beyond normal limits. I figured I was making a good first impression and left her alone for another time.

The next session began as the last one did. Piper turned her head away from me, but didn't move her feet. Her ears told me she was still not happy to see me. I fitted a rope halter to her and led her from the paddock to the arena. The horse followed a couple of steps behind me, but didn't drag too badly. When I had brushed the dust from her and picked out her hooves, I lifted the saddle onto her back. I kept a really close eye on Piper to be sure I was not going to suffer the same fate as Zoe. She looked around at me and I noticed her tail gave a couple of angry swipes. I petted her on the neck and asked her to back one step.

As I began to snug up the girth Piper swung her neck around at me, but I blocked her from making contact by lifting my elbow to greet her halfway. She then got a little fidgety and tried moving her hind end away.

THE CRANKY HORSE

I kept stroking her neck and shoulder until she stood quietly and then finished buckling the girth.

I began the session by asking her lunge around me on a 5 metre circle. At first she wanted to trot despite being asked to walk. But my persistence paid off and soon she was walking a consistent rhythm around me. However, when I asked her to walk a little bigger, there was no response. I asked again with several degrees more insistence. What I got was a nasty look with ears flat, tail whipping from side to side and a half-hearted cow kick in my direction. This time I demanded she go forward which caused her to leap in the air and take off running around me. But within two laps I got her shut down to a walk in order to try again. The next time she was more ready to go forward, but she was one seriously cranky horse about it.

After a little lunging I led her over towards the rail to collect the bridle so I could ride her. As I went to walk to the rail I felt her baulk and lean on the lead rope. I figured I needed to address this issue of not giving to the feel of the lead since it was clearly a problem. I asked her to walk with me without letting the rope get taut. When it did tighten I firmed up, walked bigger and swung the tail end of the rope behind her shoulder. I had to do this several times before she responded to the feel of the rope without waiting for the tail end to make contact with her ribs. But even though she was listening to the rope much better it was accompanied by an angry attitude. She always pinned her ears and snaked her neck in my direction. It was like she was a petulant teenager telling me "there – I did it – are you happy now – I hate you." I then worked on her back up. There is no doubt that Piper got more responsive, but there was still a drag and lateness about her work; and there was always the crankiness.

I rode her for about twenty minutes and she seemed much better under saddle than on the ground. She could still get cranky when I put more leg on her, but it wasn't as bad as when she was on the lead rope.

"Amos, can I ask you about Zoe's horse?" I had found Amos sorting out some old leather and throwing it on either the good pile or the throw away pile.

"What is it, matey?"

"She seems so unhappy. Everything I do on the ground seems to bring out the witch in her. She flattens her ears and swishes her tail. She often swings her neck as if to warn me that she is going to bite. What should I do about it?"

"Give me about 30 minutes to sort this mess out and I'll come and have a look," Amos said.

When Amos arrived at the arena he told me to show him what was going on with Piper. I went through the routine of leading her, backing her up and lunging her. She seemed especially bad when I walked into her to turn right and she tried to lunge at me with her teeth. I did my best to stay out of range and block her from making contact.

"Well, what do you think Amos?"

"Mmm, matey. I see the problem."

"Really? Well what is it?" I asked.

"Well, she thinks she's a carnivore and you've got plenty of meat on ya."

"Haha, Amos. Very funny. But what's really wrong?" I tried again.

"Okay. The problem is matey is that she's a pretty sensitive mare and a bit of a worrier. She needs a good, strong, but fair leader in her life and you ain't matchin up."

"How's that?"

"As ya know matey, all horses need leadership in their life. They depend on somebody bein the leader. If it ain't bein provided by some one else, then they have to provide it. But ya ain't doin that.

"Ya leavin Piper confused about her role in this relationship. I don't reckon ya caused it. I bet it's been a problem for a long time and why young Zoe probably got bit. But if ya gonna be workin this horse ya now have the job of fixin it."

"How Amos?"

"Matey, every time ya ask Piper to do somethin ya have to get a change of thought. It ain't enough to just get her to do the thing ya askin. Take for example when she was tryin to eat ya head off when ya tried to turn to the right. Ya got her to move her feet to the right away from ya, even though she kept tryin to bite ya. But when she was turnin to the right she never once thought to herself that she should turn right. Ya were like tryin to push a boat out to sea from the beach when the tide pushin it back in. Her brain is the tide. When the tide is pushin the boat into the beach it's hard work to get the boat out to sea. But when the tide changes and goes out, all ya gotta do is give the boat a gentle shove and the tide will carry it out. But you keep pushin against the tide. Wouldn't it better to get the tide to do the work for ya?"

"So Amos, are you saying that I need to get Piper to think about going to the right instead of pushing against her thinking about going somewhere else?"

"Yeah matey, that's right."

"But then why all the aggressiveness like ear pinning and the biting?" I asked.

"The crankiness comes from her not believin that you offer a good alternative to her own idea. Because she's sensitive and a worrier she has long ago worked out what's in her best interest and what ain't. When ya tell her to do somethin and she don't believe ya know what ya doin, then she goes into survival mode. It ain't aggression, it's protection. But it can get dangerous, like Zoe found out, because when she feels threatened she'll do what she thinks she has to so she can protect herself."

"But she's even cranky when I go to catch her. She could run away. She doesn't have to stand there if she feels so worried."

"No matey. Ya don't understand. She's been taught that she needs to stand still to be caught. She has learned that runnin gets her into more trouble. So she stands so you can halter her, but she gets cranky about it. She bit Zoe when she was bein saddled. Piper knows enough that saddlin is part of her life. But she feels bad about it and finally let Zoe know she couldn't take much more.

"The thing about a horse that is flattenin its ears or tries to nip or lifts a leg to threaten is that most people want to then punish them. They figure they'll teach 'im a lesson for threatenin them. When they do that all they are really tryin to do is train the ears not go flat or train the leg not to cow kick. They ain't doin nothin about the causes. The nippin and the ears and the tail and the cow kick tell ya somethin's wrong. But it's not them behaviours that are wrong. "

"So how should I help Piper?"

"Like me and Walt have tried to teach ya matey. Work her so that everythin ya do is about achievin softness and focus. Ask nothin of Piper that does not end with better softness and better focus. When ya ask her to turn right, keep askin 'til she gets a little softer. Don't stop just because her shoulder moved right. If ya back her up, keep repeatin enough until the back up is softer than when ya began. It ain't gotta be perfect, but it does gotta be better. Forget about the ears, the nippin and the cow kicks. The ears and nippin just tell ya got a problem the softness tells ya if it's goin away or not. Train the softness, not the ears. Pretty soon, one day you'll realize ya ain't seen her pull them ugly faces at ya for a long time and ya never did anythin about it 'cept learn to change the tide."

THE NOT SO SIMPLE ART OF HORSE TRAINING

I sometimes notice on internet forums and horse related web sites that people ask for advice on how to train a horse or correct an unwanted behaviour and even on how to break a horse in. It seems there is still a strong prevalence of opinion that training a horse in basic issues is not a very difficult or highly skilled task. In the minds of the masses teaching a horse to lead well doesn't even compare to teaching a horse to piaffe in regards to how much skill is required by the trainer. The skills to teach a horse to lead or to float load or to be broken in can be achieved by just anybody with a little experience. Yet, I have frequently had horses sent to me for float loading lessons or for bucking issues that come from very successful riders and trainers of performance horses. All of them have been horses where the basics were either badly trained or not instilled at all. There seems to be a widespread failure in the horse community to understand and appreciate the importance of excellence in the very basic skills of horsemanship. Most people think that if a horse can be led from point A to point B it leads well enough. Or a horse that is broken in to stop, go and turn is broken in well enough. This could be done by just about anybody with a bit of horsemanship experience and can be learned from books or internet advice or watching a training dvd.

Walt was leading the grey horse forward. I watched closely because I had heard Walt and Amos talking about the trouble inside this horse. Pepper seemed a pretty easygoing horse. I didn't see a whole lot of trouble in him. He didn't run around the paddock much. He wasn't very pushy to lead and he could be tied all day without moving. He was easy to catch and didn't try to crowd me at feeding time. So when I heard the old men talking about how shut down he was and the 'try' and 'preparation' were gone from him, I wasn't quite certain what they meant. But I was going to make sure that I watched as much as I could to find out. The old brothers may not have been internationally acclaimed horseman but I had learned enough that when Walt and Amos had something to say about a horse it was something worth listening to and thinking about.

As Pepper went to take the first step forward, Walt blocked him even before the foot came off the ground. The horse instantly braced up and shifted his weight back. Walt asked him forward again and again Pepper was blocked from following through with his feet. This time Walt was playing with the rope with his right hand under the horse's chin. Walt kept a tight enough grip that minute adjustments of Walt's right wrist caused Pepper to keep shifting his weight around. The horse was clearly confused and so was I.

"Amos, what is Walt asking him to do?" I asked.

"Well matey, Walt wants this little fellow to get with him," was the response.

"What do you mean?" I asked.

"Matey, the horse knows about movin forward when asked. But he don't know how to move forward and not leave. When Walt asked him to come forward, the horse was about to step a bit to the left as he came forward. That weren't what Walt was askin. He was askin to come forward, not forward and to the side. So Walt stopped it from happenin. The second ask by Walt, the horse went to the other side. He knew he was suppose to go forward, but he don't know about not leavin out to the side so since goin to the left didn't work he figured going to the right might work. Walt said no, that ain't goin to work either. Now watch."

I did watch. Walt was handling the rope under the horse's chin like it was a joystick, but with really small adjustments. I couldn't see what he was doing exactly, but I saw the horse bouncing around on the spot. A few times Pepper tried to escape by running back or leaping to the side, but Walt hung in there and got him back to the same spot without much fuss. Then after maybe three or four minutes both Walt and Pepper got very quiet – they were both virtually motionless for a moment. Then Walt asked the horse to come forward and he strode out with his head down and as straight as if he was being pulled along a wire. Walt stopped him after a few steps and rubbed him gently on the brow.

"What happened, Amos?"

"Didn't ya see it matey?"

"I don't know what I saw," I said.

"Matey, I don't know why I botha sometimes. Trainin you is like try to train a cat to play fetch!"

"Sorry Amos, but if I'm going to be a better student I need a better teacher. So what happened?"

"Well smart alec, Walt asked the horse to come forward, but the horse kept goin crooked when he came forward. Walt wouldn't let the crookedness develop. He kept blockin the horse. The little fella got confused and bothered and tried to escape a few times. He knew he had to go forward but he didn't know why Walt wouldn't let him. Finally, after the horse went through quite a struggle inside himself he got centred right down the middle of Walt's rope. Instead of his mind bouncin around left, right, back and forward, it got in the middle with Walt. There was no more escape and no more leavin, he was right there with Walt. That's when Walt let him come forward. And when he did it was as sweet, soft and focused as you could wish. That horse was right there with Walt. They were like newlyweds walking down the aisle. Walt could have led him through a bush fire or down a wombat hole."

What Walt did that day was start to build a 'try' and a 'preparation' back into that horse. The worry that caused Pepper to want to lead crooked, want to leave and not be with Walt but still be obedient and polite was being addressed. Most people I have ever seen working horses, including professionals, don't even know to think about these things. Each time Walt and Amos worked a horse they were working on building a 'try' and a 'preparation'. The approach they took was in many different forms, but the aim was always the same; to work on the inside well being of the horse in order to make the work of the horse easier and less troubling.

Most people believe that training behaviour and responses in horses is simple. The training comes down to two basic answers for most training – bigger sticks or bigger brakes. If a horse is stuck to go, get a bigger stick (spur, whip etc). If he is stuck to stop, get bigger brakes (harsher bits, martingales, running reins, hobbles, leg restraints). If he rears, use a bigger stick. If he bucks, use a bigger throttle and stick. If he doesn't tie up, reach for the bigger brakes (head collar, hobbles etc). If he is doesn't load onto a float, grab a bigger stick (bum rope, whip etc).

If you subscribe to this philosophy then training is indeed very simple. In the end you get a horse that is obedient and polite, but like Pepper, you will have a submissive and shut down horse with no 'try' and no 'preparation'. He may do what you tell him, but will he look at you when you go to rub him?

THE ONE REIN STOP

Leanne had been training her new chestnut thoroughbred for about a year when I first met her. He was an off-the-track acquisition that towered over everything else at the riding school. Leanne was a one of those people that went to every instructor and every clinician she could. She was always taking her horse to spend a lesson or even several days with somebody new. Her horse could be a little wound up and I think Leanne figured that she could always do with as much help as she could get.

I had seen her practice one rein stops on her horse. For those of you who are not familiar with them I will try to explain. A one rein stop is often referred to as an "emergency brake" and is used to get your horse to stop when he is not listening to anything else. A one rein stop is designed to stop your horse from engaging his hindquarters in a way that could nip in the bud any potential bucking, rearing, bolting or even just unwanted hyperactivity. The idea is that you use one rein to bend your horse's head to the side, which results in him yielding his hindquarters in a tight circle until he totally stops his feet moving. For example, if I use the left rein, I bring my left rein towards my hip tight enough to encourage the horse's head to come around in a tight bend to the left. He then steps his hindquarters to the right as they step around the forehand until he stops moving all together. At this point you release the rein and move on. The idea is that you practice and practice this manoeuvre until it almost becomes second nature to the horse and he does it with no resistance.

This is taught so that in the case of something untoward happening, like you feel him humping up, you ask for a one rein stop and he does it without an argument and it disperses the energy that was about to go into the buck. The secret is that you ask for a one rein stop early, when you feel something about to happen. If you wait until he is bucking or bolting chances are you are too late and you won't be able to shut it down.

So Leanne had been practicing the one rein stop religiously and her horse was so good that he would stop his feet as soon as he felt her starting to ask. Most of the time she didn't even worry about getting him to disengage his hindquarters.

I didn't know a lot about Leanne and her horse, but I knew she had been going to a local riding club every month and was really interested in horsemanship. She had attended lots of clinics with various horseman and learned about groundwork and often rode in a halter and lead rope. But when she was working on her riding and jumping she rode in a snaffle and leather reins. You could always tell what her agenda for the day was going to be by whether she wore faded blue jeans or fawn coloured jodhpurs.

It was one of those days when the weather was so perfect that you felt you could live with weather like this all year round. I was watching Amos working a young horse in the arena that he and Walt picked up at an auction. The filly had only had about five rides under Amos and she was proving to be very sensitive with a strong desire to get wherever she was going in a big hurry. It took Amos quite awhile to get her to let go of her thought to leave all the time, but after maybe forty minutes she was waiting for Amos to tell her what to do next with almost every stride. If you were to ask me what he did to change her I couldn't say because it looked like he just sat there, but I knew he was so early and ahead of her in what he asked that it didn't look like there was ever any difference between the filly's thought and Amos' thought. But Amos knew and so did the filly.

Just before Amos was about to quit his session with the horse Leanne rode into the arena for a tune up before taking him out to the cross-country paddock. I didn't take much notice of what she and her horse were doing, but I did see them go through a series of exercises that looked very much like a routine and something her horse could do in his sleep. After about fifteen minutes Amos asked me to open up the gate so he could ride his horse out of the arena and over to the paddock where he would unsaddle her. I let them out and went to close the gate and I saw Leanne's horse show signs of losing the plot. Amos had gone about twenty feet out of the gate when Leanne's horse realized Amos was leaving. There was an instant change in demeanour and what was a half sleepy horse suddenly became very alert and somewhat troubled. As his brain followed Amos' filly out the gate his feet picked up speed and started heading towards the gate. Leanne was a little slow in realizing what was happening, but managed to disengage his hindquarters before the horse got very far. I thought that would be the end of it because I knew Leanne's horse knew all about one rein stops. So I was quite surprised that he kept turning and turning without showing any sign of slowing down. In fact, he seemed to be speeding up as he turned.

Amos was watching and saw that Leanne's horse was struggling. He came back to the gate and he yelled to her to let him go a little. But Leanne was occupied with other things and didn't hear Amos. He yelled again and then again. Finally she heard him and released the reins to allow him to get a little straighter. But the instant she did he rushed towards the gate again and Leanne grabbed the rein to pull him back into a one rein stop. Again he got more worried and started to turn faster. Leanne's horse was becoming frantic and was turning so fast he was starting to trip over his own feet. Amos told me to open the gate again and he rode into the arena and right up to Leanne's spinning horse. As soon as he was aware of Amos and his horse being right there, Leanne's horse started to relax and Amos told her to let the reins out a little at a time. Finally the horse stopped turning. He was still nervous and on his toes, but he had settled enough that Leanne could jump off. Amos held her horse while she calmed down and allowed her jelly legs to regain some of their strength. Amos ponied her horse out of the arena and over to her stable where Leanne unsaddled him.

Later Leanne came looking for Amos to thank him for his help.

"Thanks Amos. It was lucky you were there," she said.

"Well, it wouldn't have happened if I had not bin there."

"I guess I had better do more work on the one rein stop. I thought we had them good enough that we could handle any emergencies like that one," she said.

"Well young lady, ya got them good enough. But them one rein stops ain't always the answer and sometimes they're the problem," Amos responded.

"But I thought they were meant to stop a horse who was about to freak out, Amos. They've worked before. Are you saying they don't work?" she asked.

"Oh, they can work okay in the right situation. But ya gotta know when the right situation is. They ain't for every situation. There are two problems with usin one rein stops and ya found one them today," he said.

"My instructor never said anything about being careful when to use them. He said to they were useful in any situation," Leanne asked.

"Well for instance, what happened today? Ya horse decided he needed to be with my horse. It was more than just important to him it was life and death. He needed to be goin out the gate with us. He is so insecure that he knew he might die if he was left in that arena with only you to help him. So when he tries to go with us ya turn him around and try to make him stop movin. Now he believes he must move and you tell him he can't move. So now ya in a battle between him tryin to save his life and you tellin him ya don't care about his life as long as he don't move. This ain't gonna change nothin for the betta. He's naturally gonna get more desperate and that's what happened. The more insistent ya got about tellin him he can't head towards the gate, the more panicked he got and the faster he turned. If ya had kept it up he was goin to either fall over or try to unload ya."

"What should I have done then Amos?"

"Well, ya might have allowed him to move, but direct his movement. Don't tell a horse who has to move that he can't move, but direct his movement. That way ya not goin to get him in as big a panic. And when ya ask him to turn, direct his front end to turn and not his hindquarters. If ya try to steer the rear end with disengagements he will think ya tryin to get him to stand still. But ask his forehand to follow the rein and turn him just tight enough that his encourages him to at least not get faster or even

THE ONE REIN STOP

betta he might slow down. When he does slow down, let him go. He will get quick again when he sees the gate, but turn his forehand again in a circle that helps him slow his feet and his thoughts then let him go. Don't try to keep control of his speed by turning and turning, let him get it wrong again and fix it. Ya probably will have do this over and over again for a long time the first time before he changes his mind about the gate and another horse. But if ya stick with it he will change and he will feel betta for it and ya won't run the risk of gettin dumped."

I then chimed in with a question.

"So what's the second problem with a one rein stop Amos?"

"The second problem matey is that because ya is askin a horse to stand still with his head turned around, ya breakin the connection between the rein and his feet. The reins are there to direct his feet. Every time ya pick up a rein and ask his head to turn but his feet don't, ya teachin a horse not to be accurate to the reins. One day ya might be goin somewhere and ya need to turn him, but he don't want to turn. Ya will probably be able to get his head around, but his feet might keep goin in the same direction. It ain't any fun ridin a rubber necked horse. Believe me mate. There'll be plenty a rides where ya'll be thankful ya horse is goin where he is nose is pointin. "

Even today the one rein stop is taught as if it is the magic answer to any sort of trouble in a horse. But in some cases it will cause more problems than it can solve. By all means teach your horse how to disengage his hindquarters in response to one rein. But there is almost never a good reason why you'd insist him to stop moving in order to regain control. A horse will give you back control as his panic subsides and this is best done by allowing him to move his feet while directing them – not stopping them.

BARRY AND CEDAR

Barry was a fellow in his late thirties who trained horses. He recently arrived at the riding school where he set up his business temporarily while he looked around for a property to buy. He told me that he had been working in Western Australia for most of his life, but after his divorce his wife got the farm and he decided to move east. Barry sometimes asked me to help with a horse or two when he needed an extra rider. I was happy to oblige because I was always looking for more experience and I thought it might be possible to learn something from Barry that I hadn't learned from Walt or Amos.

One of Barry's clients had a buckskin called Cedar. He was with Barry because the owner found it difficult to control Cedar when she rode out with other horses. It seems that Cedar always wanted to be in front and would lose the plot if another horse went ahead. Barry asked if I would help out by riding his older horse, Precious, when he rode Cedar down the trail.

For the first few days Barry worked Cedar exclusively in the arena. He explained that with a problem like Cedar's it was inevitably a failure of the stop command. He said he needed to instil in Cedar that stopping in response to the reins and seat was not something that Cedar needed to debate. Stop meant stop and no other interpretation should be tolerated. Once a horse understood that he must stop when asked, Barry said a problem such as Cedar's would just go away. He explained to me that on any horse the basics of stopping, going and turning needed to be so good and so clear that obedience to them overrode any desire that a horse may have to argue with them. I was fascinated by this philosophy. It was simple and logical. He further went on to explain that basic principles that governed a horse's actions were the same in every horse no matter how sensitive or dull, smart or slow they were. The difference between horses was not in what was the most effective method for any particular horse, but in how much pressure to apply and how often it needs to be repeated with any given method. He said that instead of using different methods on different horses, if you use a method whose principles were consistent with how a horse learns then the only decision you need to make in applying a method is how much pressure and the number of repetitions to use. Walt and Amos had never explained training in so simple a way. I knew I was going to learn a lot from Barry.

A little over a week had passed since Cedar first arrived. Barry seemed pretty happy with the way Cedar was working and his response to the reins was dramatically improved. It was time to go on a trail ride with Precious.

We started out riding side by side, but Cedar wanted to push ahead. Barry managed to keep him along side Precious. We stopped a few times because Barry wanted to check that Cedar was listening to the reins. The stop button seemed to be working so far. Next Barry told me to ride ahead, so I asked Precious to trot out. This was all very new to me so I didn't realize I wasn't suppose to leave in such a hurry or go so far. I heard a voice and I looked back and I saw Barry struggling to settle Cedar. He had the reins fairly short and Cedar was prancing sideways. I saw Barry firm up on the reins and ask Cedar to backup. His horse took a few steps back then planted his feet. Barry asked more and Cedar reared vertically. When Cedar's feet returned to earth Barry kicked him forward and after a few strides, demanded a stop. Cedar ran backwards and fell on his hind end. When he recovered, Cedar was prancing all over the trail. Barry called for me to return in order to help get Cedar settled again. It didn't take long for Cedar to recover with Precious walking alongside him.

Barry then asked me to go ahead of him again, but this time I was to only walk Precious and stop just fifty metres away. Cedar did fine until we got about thirty metres away when he started prancing sideway. Barry asked him to stop, but Cedar did a half rear, then another and another. Barry tried to back him up, but Cedar just put more energy into rearing. It was clear Barry and I that more work at home was needed. So we called it quits for that day and headed home together. When we got back to the riding school, Barry took Cedar into the arena and worked him hard – with particular attention to his halts and rein back, which were both really good. The next day we tried it again, but despite Cedar working well in the arena and despite me being more careful not to take Precious too far or too fast from Cedar, the result was the same. The situation was clearly a little trickier than Barry had thought. I wanted to suggest he talk to Walt for an opinion, but I got the feeling that Barry would not be very open to such a idea.

Barry continued to ride Cedar in the arena and in the paddock and I helped him on Precious. Everything was fine as long as we did not leave the front gate of the riding school. But no amount of effort on Barry's part to improve the stop button made much improvement on Cedar when he was taken for a trail ride.

A week or so after I started helping Barry, Walt came to ask me if I could help him to pick up feed at the store. When we were motoring along in the old Ford truck Walt asked me how things were going with Cedar and Barry. At the time I didn't realize it, but Walt already knew the answer to that question. I told him all about what had been happening. I told him that Barry had been concentrating on getting Cedar obedient to the stop command. All was well until Cedar was out on the trail when he seemed to forget all about the stop.

"Well matey, I don't think Cedar actually forgets about stoppin. It's just that he's actually got other things on his mind that seem more important to him."

"But Walt, Barry reckons that a horse must be so good with the stop, go and turn buttons that when asked, they override anything else a horse might do."

"Matey, that might be ok when the sun is shining and the birds is singin and all is right with the world from the horse's point of view. But no amount of trainin is goin to override a horse's need to survive. It's the most important instinct a horse has and if ya try to train him to do somethin that he thinks is goin to put him in jeopardy then all ya trainin is goin to be for nothin."

I thought about that for a few moments.

"So you don't think improving his stop to the reins is going to help?" I asked.

"Matey, for some horses that just like to be in front askin them to slow up or stop might be just fine. But for a horse like Cedar that reckons his life depends on bein in front, it might be too much to ask him to stop and stay back."

"Walt, Barry says that all horses learn the same and it's just a matter of how much pressure and how many times you have to repeat it. But you're saying that's not true. I'm confused!"

"Well matey, if you wanna know which to believe ask yourself how it is workin for Cedar right now?"

We talked some more in the truck about how Cedar could be helped with his problem and Walt gave me some ideas to think about. That afternoon I went to Barry and talked to him about some of things that Walt had suggested. At first he was a little miffed and argued some points, but in the end I asked him what did he have to lose by trying a different approach? I even suggested that we ask Walt to ride out with us the next day. That way Walt's input would be first hand rather that our interpretation of what I thought he said.

Walt rode Burner, I rode Precious and Barry rode Cedar. It was a beautiful day and the horses were feeling very mellow. When we got to the part where Walt and I took our horses away from Cedar, things fell apart in a hurry. Walt coached on Barry to turn Cedar with a bend, but Barry didn't really understand what Walt was trying to get him to do. Walt and I returned to Barry's side to help settle Cedar down and then Walt asked if he could ride Cedar. Barry was a little hesitant because he didn't want the old man getting hurt. But Walt was not going to be refused.

Walt got aboard Cedar and checked out the feel of the reins. After he was satisfied with what he felt he suggested that Barry and I walk our horses on ahead. We only got about thirty feet when Cedar started to get anxious to be with us. Walt picked up the left rein and held it out past his knee. This tipped Cedar's nose to the left. Cedar continued to try to head our way, but Walt tightened the rein even further to the left and eventually Cedar's feet spun to the left. Walt released the rein just as Cedar's feet gave to going left. But quick as a flash Cedar turned a full circle and was heading towards Barry and me. Still the old man's timing was superb and he picked up the right rein and held it further past his knee until Cedar gave and turned his feet to the right nearly running them both into a tree. When Walt released the rein he allowed Cedar to wander back towards us, but just as Cedar started to hurry Walt was right there to bend him to the left again until his feet stopped hurrying. When Cedar was turning with a slightly more relaxed walk, Walt let go of the rein and allowed Cedar to wander towards us again. It was a wonderful display of timing and feel. Every time Cedar got hurried, Walt bent him to a calmer walk and then allowed Cedar to find his own way back to us.

After about ten minutes Cedar was walking calmly behind us. With this breakthrough Walt asked Barry and I to bring our horses back to Cedar and we walked together for a few minutes. Then Walt had us trot up ahead for about 100 yards. When Cedar started to rush Walt went back to bending him to a walk and then allowing him to wander back in our direction. Pretty soon, Barry and I were able to trot our horses away without Cedar rushing to join us. It was clear to both Barry and I that this was the breakthrough that Barry had been aiming for, but kept missing.

On the ride back to the riding school I asked Walt, "How come you didn't keep turning Cedar until he stopped? You turned him and then let him go and then turned him again. But he never stopped. Why?"

"Well matey, there was a desperation in the horse to move. His worry wouldn't let his feet be still. Barry found that himself when he tried to stop him and the horse reared. By allowin him move, but keepin it under control with the turns, I was lettin some of the worry leak out of the horse. When Cedar slowed his feet a little it told me he was startin to change some of them bad feelins, so it was okay for him to head towards your horses. But when he lost track of me and the nice walk and stated to hurry again, I turned him until he remembered to let go of some of that worry."

In reality, Cedar's problem had nothing to do with how good his stop button was operating. It was all to do with Cedar's perception of how safe he was trailing behind other horses when away from home. I think Barry and I both learned that different horses do have different needs that require different approaches. If you try to apply a mechanistic approach to something that is not a mechanism, somewhere along the line you are going to run into horses that you can't help.

IT FELT RIGHT AT THE TIME

Occasionally Walt and Amos would take me with them to the horse sales. It was usual for the old brothers to look out for a bargain. They would bring one or two home, train it up for a few weeks or months and then sell it on to a suitable home. It was their way of supplementing their pension cheques. They had been doing this for much longer than I had been alive and they had developed a good eye for horses. I had never seen them buy a dud that caused them to lose money. I guess they figured that part of my education should be to learn how to go about choosing a good horse.

    The sale yard was not very big. There was a large pen where the horses were either ridden or paraded and there were about 30 other smaller pens to hold maybe 80 horses. All the yards were held together with bailing twine and rope, with only the occasional nail or bolt to give the appearance of solidity. The auctioneer walked from pen to pen along an overhead walkway that seemed to barely support his rotund frame. I have to say that my most lingering impression from those days was the characters that attended each month. Most would fit comfortably into a Dickens story about down trodden London. Some of them made the old brothers appear almost aristocratic.

    On one visit to the monthly sale neither Walt nor Amos saw anything they felt was worth their time in buying. I had noticed a bay gelding that was standing among a group of four horses. He was around 15 hh and had a stocky build. But he looked to have the worst hair-day of his life. Despite it being spring he looked like a woolly mammoth on valium.

I brought the horse to Amos' attention. He studied it for a bit, checked the teeth, ran a hand down his legs, picked up the feet and examined the mane and ears.

"Matey, he is about 9 years old and a good strong build, but he is in a bad way. He is way under condition. Those feet are swollen badly 'cause he's got mud fever. His back is scabbed due to rain scald and he is covered in lice. The poor fellow has been badly neglected and those feet will take a bit of work to get him moving properly."

"But Amos he does seem a nice type and would make somebody a good riding horse wouldn't he," I asked?

"Sure matey. He seems a nice type, but it will take so much work to get him right that to make a profit on him he would have to almost be given away today."

"Well can we wait a bit and see? He might be really cheap and I will do all the work for you to clean him up and get him going," I pleaded.

Walt came over to see what the trouble was about. Amos told him that we were waiting to see what the bay gelding went for. He said the "boy's got his heart on gettin him right and if he is cheap enough he might be a good buy."

Walt just shook his head and mumbled something about not being a charity.

The gelding got passed in without a single bid. Amos went up to the seller and offered him $20 for the horse. The fellow looked shocked. But when Amos told him $35, take it or leave it, the fellow said that it will at least pay his petrol and he sure didn't want to take the horse home again.

I couldn't have been more pleased with myself. Even though the horse belonged to Amos and Walt I felt I had just bought my first horse.

Amos told me to get a halter from the truck and lead the horse over there while he settled with the owner. I led the horse over to the truck as Walt was lowering the tailgate. I knew that one of the first projects would be to teach him to lead better because it was taking quite an effort to drag him to the parking lot. When we finally got there Walt told me to lead him up the ramp. That seemed like a good idea at the time except nobody told the gelding. He figured that his feet were not going up any ramp – especially one that led him into a tin cave.

"Just keep asking him matey," were Walt's words of encouragement.

I slapped my leg with the tail end of the lead rope, but the horse just stood like a sentry. If anything he leaned harder against the rope. When I asked more insistently the horse leapt to my left and braced up to bolt off. I just managed to turn him back to face the ramp, but it took nearly all my strength. I went to ask him forward again when I heard Walt's voice.

"Whooaa matey. Just pet 'im. Wait a bit and rub on 'im."

I did as Walt said, but I wasn't sure why I should pet a horse that just tried to take off on me.

"There. See how he let down a smidge? Now matey ask 'im again to come forward."

I did as Walt said. He took another step towards the ramp. I stopped and petted him again. I repeated this all the way to the foot of the ramp. But when it came time to ask him to step up on the ramp of the truck he reared then ran backwards. I kept trying to ask him to come forward, but I heard Walt yelling at me to go with him instead. It took me a second or two to get the idea to not pull on the rope, but allow slack in it as the horse ran backwards. Soon the horse just stopped and looked at me as if to ask how did we both got here?

I don't mind admitting today that I was more than a little perplexed about what was going on. I had seen Walt load enough troubled horses to know that he can get pretty insistent on them coming forward and not stop asking them until they did take a step forward. But here was a case when Walt was having me ease off if the horse ran back and I didn't know why.

When the gelding seemed to have hit another soft spot I stopped petting him and asked him forward again. This time he managed to take a step onto the ramp, but then I felt him lean back. Unfortunately, I was just too late to ease the pressure off the rope and the little fellow bolted backwards again. I did my best to keep up with him and not allow the slack to come out of the rope until he stopped. Again I rubbed him softly until he hit a relaxed spot and brought him forward to the ramp. He took one step onto the ramp and just as he was about to lean back again I let the rope go slack and petted him.

"That was okay matey, now wait a moment," Walt said.

I kept petting him and just as I was about to ask him forward again Walt said, "now, matey lead 'im over to that grass over there and let him have a pick. When he's done he'll go on with no trouble."

I looked at Walt with a dumbfound expression that he chose to ignore.

"Go on, matey. He'll be okay."

I did as I was told and after maybe two or three minutes Walt told me to lead the horse onto the truck. This time the little bay walked quietly to the foot of the ramp, hesitated for half a second and then walked right into the back of the truck. I couldn't have been more surprised than if the horse had asked for the time of day.

I got the back locked up just as Amos appeared and we all loaded into the truck.

I knew Walt knew something about that horse that I had missed. I wanted to know how he knew to let the horse graze for a minute or two.

"Walt, why did you have me walk the horse over to the grass to eat?"

"Oh, I don't know matey. It seemed like the right thing to do."

Aaaggghhh! That was not an answer. That didn't tell me anything. I needed to know. I needed to know what Walt knew!

"That doesn't tell me anything Walt. What did you see that told you it was the right thing to do?"

"Matey, when ya look at a friend and see he's in trouble, how do ya know how to help him? Ya do what feels right. It's the same with a horse. It ain't no different.

"But how do you know what feels right to a horse," I asked?

"Ya look at 'im like a friend. Ya can read all the books and talk to all the best trainers and they will tell ya to do this and to do that. But none of them books and none of them trainers can tell ya what's ailin ya horse if they ain't spent time with 'im. If ya learn to think of a horse as a friend, ya can figure out pretty much everythin ya need to know to help 'im. Ya just learn to feel what's right for 'im."

I was expecting a logical and rational explanation from Walt and I should have known better. But feeling what was best at the time has helped me learn a lot about the inner workings of a horse's emotions and needs. It has kept me from falling into the pattern of using a "method". Sometimes I have got it wrong and had to re-think an approach, but that's just another reminder that I have a long way to go and another experience to draw from for the next horse.

WALT AND THE FOAL

"Matey, d'ya have an hour tomorrow afternoon to give me a hand. I need a little help holdin a mare while I try to catch a foal. Amos' back is playin up again and he's cryin about havin to help."

"Yeah I think I can help, Walt. I should finish the stables by about two if that suits you," I said.

"That'll work, matey. It's only a few miles down the road so I'll meet ya by the truck when ya get finished."

The next afternoon Walt was waiting for me in the truck. He was listening to the cricket on a little transistor radio that he always carried when a test match was playing. After I got settled in the truck and Chappell had survived another over by Michael Holding, Walt fired up the old Ford. We trundled down the road as the truck complained about its intestinal problems the whole way.

We got to the farm and found the mare and foal had been put into a yard that was almost a small paddock. Walt managed to catch the mare with no problem, but the chestnut colt was not as happy about being caught as mum. Walt decided that given the limited time he had no choice but to throw a rope on the little fellow. He collected an old lariat made from rawhide. It looked like it had been used by Noah to bring in all the animals two by two. Walt made a loop and without even setting up a swing he tossed it high and watched as it floated down and over the neck of the colt. I had never seen an animal roped so smoothly. Normally there was a lot of swinging of the rope and dust from the panicked prey before anything was caught. But Walt just kept everything low key and easy. The colt didn't even get a chance to run for his life before he was caught. But once he felt the rope around his neck he took off without a thought. Walt kept the rope feeding out so as not to pull on the colt and soon the foal stopped running.

Walt waited for a bit before slowly walking towards the foal's shoulder and coiling his rope at the same time. As he got within about five feet of the colt, the foal took off again. This time Walt held fast and the colt hit the end of the lariat and spun around looking at Walt and wondering how that happened. Walt waited another minute to let the foal soak on the events before again taking a few steps towards him. The foal thought about taking off and but this time Walt saw it happening before it happened and stepped back. It gave the young one more room and took the pressure off. The process of approaching the foal repeated itself several times with Walt backing away just before the foal decided to leave. After perhaps ten minutes Walt was standing by the foal's shoulder and rubbing his face.

Walt asked me to hand him the baby halter. He slipped it on the foal who seemed almost nonchalant about his new accessory. Walt's hands began to explore the neck and body of the foal in a way that seemed reassuring. Whenever the colt tensed to tell Walt that he was approaching a 'no go' area, Walt eased off for a moment and soon that 'no go' became an 'ok' area. Steadily Walt worked along the side and back of the foal and was able to touch him all over his body. He bent to pass his hand down the left hind leg in a smooth swipe. The foal picked up his leg as if to walk away, but Walt just followed him until he stood again. Walt went to back to work touching the legs and it only took about five minutes before he could touch all the legs, his body, ears, muzzle and chest.

Next Walt took the halter off, but kept the lariat around the foal's neck. He stepped a away a few feet from the foal and then approached him again with his hand ready to rub his neck. The foal flinched as if to move away, but settled immediately Walt's hand touched him. Again, Walt moved away and this time approached the foal ready to fit the halter. Initially there was some head tossing in an attempt to avoid the noseband, but Walt steadied him with his hand over the bridge of the colt's nose. Next time Walt walked about ten feet away before approaching again. Following that he walked twenty feet before turning to walk up to the foal to be caught. When the little fellow went to leave Walt steadied him with the lariat and the foal accepted Walt's presence readily. About five minutes later Walt took the lariat from around the colt's neck and walked to the other end of the pen. The foal watched him closely, but when he figured all was safe he went to mum for a drink. Walt then approached the foal with the halter and caught him with no problem at all.

"I think matey that's pretty good for the first day. Tomorrow if ya got time to help I think we can start leadin and get them feet picked up."

"Okay, I can help Walt. I haven't seen a foal halter started before. It's so interesting, but not unlike what you might do with an older horse, do you think?"

"Ya right, it is kinda like that. But ya have to remember that most foals are no more than frightened and that's why they sometimes do the wrong thing. But an older horse might be spoiled and taught to do the wrong thing by being messed around by people. Older horses have habits, but most foals ain't got habits. Foals usually ain't had enough handlin to be messed up by folk," Walt said.

"Well it looked to me Walt, that this colt is very quick to catch on. Is that normal?"

"Matey, most foals are quick learners. They have the advantage of not already knowin a whole lot of bad stuff that somebody has taught them and then gets in the way of them learnin. If it's done right ya can teach a foal somethin that might take an older horse four times longer to learn.

The other thing to keep in mind is that when ya teach a horse somethin for the first time, when it's his first experience of that thing, it is the experience that he will most remember. He will always revert back to what he knew when he was first taught. So ya gotta make sure that his first experience is the one ya want him to retain. If ya teach him to be afraid or to be resistant or to not focus or whatever, ya will always be workin to make sure he don't go back to that. But if from the very start he learns to be soft, responsive and relaxed and to have a try, even if some fool comes along and messes it all up later it won't be too hard to get it all back. It will be what he knows best."

"That's a lot of responsibility, Walt," I observed.

"You bet matey. But when ya are responsible for somethin that has feelins it's always a big responsibility. It's goin to be interestin to see this little colt in a years' time or three years' time. Right now he has no bad history and he is curious enough about the world and people to want to try to understand his place in it. That's why he is such a quick learner. But d'ya reckon he will be just as interested and have just as much try in three years' time when he gets broken in? I doubt it. By the time he gets started I bet the owner will have killed most of the try in him. She won't mean to do it, but somehow horse people don't know how not to. It's sad, but it just seems to be the way things are.

C'mon matey, let's go. I wish ya knew how to drive so I could listen to the cricket on the way back. Chappell is probably out by now."

NONE OF YOUR BEESWAX

When Anne first came to board at the riding school she had two horses. One was about eight years old and had been her regular riding horse for the last three years. She took him on the occasional trail ride, but his main job was to win her ribbons at the local shows. Anne's second horse was an unbroken two and half year old gelding called Beeswax. I think Anne told me once that he got the name when he was just a little fellow. He was always so curious around people and getting his nose into their pockets or buckets or cars etc. One day he even started to explore under Anne's mother's skirt. After her initial shock at this intrusion, Anne's mother curtly told him that what was under there was none of his beeswax. Thus the name!

There was no doubt about it; Beeswax was a curious fellow with a ton of personality. As part of my responsibilities at the riding school I was required to clean paddocks. Anytime I would go into Beeswax's paddock it was an interesting experience. Not only would he follow me around, but he would love to show off too. Sometimes, he would gallop full pelt around the perimeter and then leap into the air with four feet off the ground, then he would run some more followed by another giant leap. This could continue until exhaustion overcame him. On other occasions he would shadow me around, nudge the wheelbarrow to turn it over when my back was turned or he would pick up a stick in his mouth and throw it in the air sometimes landing on my head or his head. He even learned to play chasing with me. This began one day when I was cleaning the paddock. I stopped to scratch him really roughly on his chest (his favourite way to be petted). Before I knew what was happening he grabbed my hat and trotted off. I chased him at a half run. Beeswax waited until I almost got to him then he trotted off a further distance and waited for me to catch up. I remember him looking so smug standing there waiting for me with his head up, tail up and my hat in his mouth. This game went on for a few minutes until I was able to snatch the hat out of his mouth. When I put it on my head and turned to go back to my duties he trotted on tiptoes right behind me in his best Peppy Le Pew impersonation. This was a game that we played many times over the months.

Another favourite game for Beeswax was to pick up anything left on the gate and drag it around the paddock. It could be a halter, a rug, lead rope, anything. If a person was in the paddock he would drag the object over to them and drop it like a dog wanting to play fetch. If they put it back on the gate he would pick it up again and bring it right back. I even saw him carry a lead rope in his mouth and fling his head in such a way that the rope spun in a circle. Beeswax was able to pick up on the rhythm of his head tossing and after very little effort he was able to repeat the rope twirl. He seemed so pleased with himself and I saw him do this many times. I had never seen such a thing before. Beeswax was certainly one out of the box. He and I became great friends over the months he was at the riding school.

Eventually, it came time for Anne to start Beeswax under saddle. She had been having some behaviour problems with her older horse and felt that Beeswax was going to make a better riding prospect in the show ring. I had to agree that he was a good looking horse and people couldn't help but notice his personality and pizzazz which I figured would be a plus in any competition event.

Since Beeswax and I had become such good mates I was very interested to see how he would go with the breaking in process. Anne said she didn't mind if I watched occasionally. Up to then most of my experience of horse breaking was from Walt and Amos and what they had taught me. I had seen a couple of other people and had started a few horses myself by this stage, but I knew I still had so much to learn that I thought it would be a good learning experience to watch Anne with Beeswax.

NONE OF YOUR BEESWAX

What I saw was very different from what I had learned from Walt and Amos. Anne started by putting Beeswax in the round yard with a roller on his back. The roller didn't cause him much concern. The worse thing he did was to try to turn his head to bite on the girth leathers. Next came the bridle. Anne bridled him and fitted a tie down. The reins of the tie down went from the girth of the roller, through the rings of the bit and back to the rings on the back of the roller. The reins were fairly loosely fitted and didn't confine Beeswax at all. Anne sat and watched Beeswax sort out this situation for about half and hour. After that she shortened the reins a few inches and again left him to sort it out. Over about a three hour period Anne tightened the reins several times before taking all the gear off and putting him back in the paddock. I didn't understand what she was doing, but she later told me that was the way to mouth a horse. Anne repeated the process for the next three days and each time the reins were shortened more and more. By the end of the third hour of the third day Beeswax was wandering around the round yard with his nose almost to his chest. I noticed the corners of his lips were red raw.

This mouthing procedure was followed by a couple of days of tying Beeswax's head to one side using only one rein. Again, over a period of time the rein was tightened little by little. It was repeated on the other side too. After all this mouthing, Beeswax was long reined around the round yard with the tie down fitted. By the third day of long reining he was saddled and lunged with the tie down still in place. The next day Anne hoped on board of Beeswax with the help of a friend. Beeswax was a perfect gentleman and didn't provide any reason for Anne's blood pressure to elevate. The following day Anne rode him while her friend lunged him in the round pen. Again, he was well behaved although he travelled in an over bent and hollow fashion. In the days that followed Anne was able to ride him more and more. She swapped the tie down for a running martingale. A couple of weeks after Anne began to break in Beeswax she was proudly riding him around the property and he behaved like he had been doing it for years. I noticed he was always riding over bent with a hollow back and his hindquarters trailing way behind, but he was well behaved.

About the same time something else seemed to be happening to Beeswax. There was a change in the way he was in the paddock. I would go into the paddock and he would hardly acknowledge me. Where once he would run over to play and be a royal pain in the behind, he more and more seemed very aloof. He used to approach me for a scratch on his chest, but he wouldn't come looking for the scratches. And as for playing chasings, it never happened anymore.

I told Anne about this and asked if she had noticed anything different about him. She said he seemed fine to her and he was not off his feed or lame. She said that maybe now that he is broken in that his brain has matured from playing like a kid to thinking like an adult. I wondered about this and decided to ask Walt.

"Well matey, it's true that Beeswax is getting older and growing up, but that ain't why he ain't wantin to play with ya anymore. If ya notice him in the paddock when nobody's with him he's still the same character looking for mischief he always was. The only thing that's changed is how he feels about dealin with people."

"But why, Walt?" I asked

"Well matey, while he was gettin broken in a lot of his choices was taken away from him. A lot of the things he was taught was taught to him by makin him give in and sort of forced on him. It wasn't a matter that Beeswax was taught that people had good ideas. He was taught that people had the only ideas that ought to matter to him and if he didn't agree then he was in for more discomfort."

"What do you mean?" I asked looking for a clearer explanation.

"Beeswax had his head tied down in order to teach him to give to the bit. But if the truth were really known he was taught that the bit was a source of pain and he could do nothin about it. Could you imagine how sore ya'd be if I tied ya head down like that for three hours a day? You'd fight it until the fightin caused you more pain and you'd give to the bit. Then eventually ya muscles would get sore and cramped from havin ya neck bent, so you'd lean on that bit harder again until the pain in ya mouth was worse than the pain in ya neck. It's a no win situation for ya and eventually ya just give up the fight and try to tune the pain and discomfort out. That's what Beeswax learned to do. He's learned to go along with the discomfort and not fight it, but in order to do that he has also learned to tune out to people. The spark and personality that was

Beeswax has been pushed deep down inside himself by a trainin method that gave him no choices that he could be happy with. There is a difference between makin somethin hard for a horse and makin it impossible. Makin the wrong thing hard and the right thing easy gives a horse a choice where if he chooses the human's idea he will find a sweet spot. But makin the wrong thing impossible and the right thing only a little less impossible means there is no sweet spot for the horse to find that he can be happy about. It kills the essence of the horse. That's what breakin in Beeswax has done. It's killed his spirit. It's a sad thing to see, matey."

Beeswax went on to become Anne's main riding horse. She took him to club rallies and competitions and he performed pretty well according to the ribbons she took home. Beeswax never did regain that sparkle in the time I knew him. I really missed my old friend. About three years later I heard that he suffered ongoing back and hindquarter problems. I wondered if Anne's next horse would fare better.

THE ROUTINE OF CHANGE

I watched Walt riding a horse in the arena. The owner was watching too. After about 15 minutes he said to her that he was going to see how he goes down the road.

"Do you want me to open the gate?" she asked.

No, don't worry about it. He can do it. It'll be a good job for him," Walt replied.

He rode Perry along the rail of the arena and parked him next to the gate. His hip touched the gate and he swung to the side. Walt put him back next to the gate and patted him. Then he leaned over to rattle the gate and again Perry swung away. Again the old man put him back. He reached for the gate again and stroked him at the same time. Perry stood quietly while Walt lifted the latch and let the gate swing open. Perry tried to immediately head through the gate, but Walt stopped him, waited for him to soften then turned him in the opposite direction and walked away from the gate. After a few metres Walt turned him back to the gate and asked him to stand quietly. When his brain had stopped trying to get his feet through the gate Walt asked him to walk out of the arena. He rode him down the driveway and out of the property. The owner and I followed on foot as Walt and Perry rode down the tree-lined road.

Along the way they found puddles to splash through, embankments to climb up and down, trees to squeeze between, horses to chase them along the fence line and cars to whiz past. Some of these things Perry had more trouble with than others. The puddles seemed an almost insurmountable obstacle at first, but given the time he needed to explore the water, Perry found his boldness and made enough splash on the way through to soak both he and the old man. The cars and embankments were not a problem, but squeezing between the trees was a little more challenging. Nevertheless, when they got back to the saddling rail and Perry was given plenty of praise.

"I reckon he did pretty good for his first trail ride," Walt told the owner.

"He was great," she said! "I would never have thought he would be so good. Even opening the gate was different. If anything touched his hip like that gate did he would normally have had a bucking fit. And he hates water. I was always too afraid to take him on a trail ride because he was so spooky and when he spooked he bucked."

"You mean you never took him out on a trail?" Walt asked.

"No. He was too unpredictable. I always just rode him in the arena and even then it didn't feel safe."

The lady had bred Perry and broken him in herself. He was now six years old and been ridden for three years, yet he had never been on a trail, opened a gate or ridden through a puddle.

Part of Perry's problem is that his life consisted of routines. He lived in the same paddock with the same companions. He was fed the same time each day. He was ridden the same days each week at about the same time in the same arena. He did the same exercises for the same length of time and then put back in the same paddock. Perry had become bored and frustrated. If anything out of the ordinary happened, like another horse rode past the arena, he would act like his life was in danger and scoot and buck. The owner's safety depended on Perry's life staying routine.

The next time the owner came to visit she was shocked to see me leading Perry from the paddock while I rode the four-wheel motorbike. Perry trotted alongside happily keeping up as I turned the corner, got off and opened the gate and sped off again just expecting that Perry was going to come along – which he did. I tied him to a post outside the arena while Walt went to get the saddle and tack. The boss's wife was working a horse in the round pen, which was of great interest to Perry who handled it like a spectator at a tennis match.

Once Walt had Perry saddled and ready to ride he climbed the fence of the yard like a monkey and asked Perry to sidle up alongside for him to step aboard. Perry was only 14.2 and Walt certainly didn't need a stepladder to get on, but this was another thing the horse had never done and so it was a good opportunity. At first Perry kept swinging his hindquarters away as Walt tried to get him in position for to throw a leg over. But with a little persistence he finally was in the perfect position for the old man to mount.

They rode a circle and then told the owner they were going to the arena. She went to open the gate to the laneway, but Walt told her he was going to take a shortcut through the barn. Going through the barn allowed them to bypass the laneways and led straight to the driveway that led to the arena. On this day the barn had a horse float parked inside, a John Deere gator parked behind the float and a horse tied up outside one of the stables. Perry was pretty unsure about riding through the 2 metre gap between the stable door and the horse float. But once he achieved that terrifying task it was no problem to go around the gator and behind the tied up horse. The owner later told me it was Perry's first time under a roof since he was weaned.

When Perry went home he was a pretty settled horse and his experiences of life had expanded exponentially. He had been tied up for hours. He had been ridden to the letterbox and asked to stand while Walt collected the mail. He had chased the quad bike while being ridden. He had opened a couple of dozen gates. He even got to ride over a see-saw and balance in the middle tipping it up and down. Perry's whole world now consisted of many new and interesting situations. Some of them were hard and some were easy, but they all added to making Perry a better and happier horse.

It is interesting to me how we can limit our horse's potential by trying to protect them and ourselves from things that might be frightening. No horse feels better being protected. It means he has to spend the rest of his days feeling he needs protection. If I am going to present a challenge to my horse all I have to ask myself is will he be able to try and will he be better for having tried? If the answer is, no, to both of those questions then I don't even go there. But if it is yes, then I know I am doing him a favour.

The more we expose our horses to the things that might bother them and the outcome is a good one, the better they will be. The only routine we should offer our horses is the routine of change. But like everything in horsemanship, the important thing is not whether the horse does what we want, but whether he is a better horse for trying it.

FERRET GRASS

Every year I hear about the trouble people have with their horses because of spring grass. It seems all that extra sugar and protein in the grass has the ability to turn poor little Dobbin into a fire-breathing monster whose only purpose in life is to wipe out anyone who comes near him. The same is often said of mares that come into season, colts that have serviced a mare and any horse that has been fed too much lucerne (alfalfa). I have seen enough horses to know that these things are real and people struggle with these issues. But the reason why these problems arise has been a consideration of mine for a long time.

We had a new boarder at the riding school called Beth-Anne. She was in her early thirties and had just got back into riding after a break of several years. Her new horse was a thoroughbred called Diplomacy Ascot or Dipper for short, who had retired from racing only six months earlier. At first he was a bit of a handful for Beth-Anne. He was prone to prancing sideways and would often throw his head up high whenever she lifted the reins. But with the help of a local instructor over several months, Beth-Anne and Dipper began to look more like a team. He was softer in his mind and body and was less prone to getting uptight when other horses came near him or when ridden out of the arena. The progress was looking pretty good and Beth-Anne certainly was pleased.

The riding school was usually pretty busy on a Saturday morning. I remember one Saturday I was walking past a group of boarders that were talking to each other. I heard Beth-Anne telling a few people that Dipper was back to his old tricks again. She said when she rode him in the arena he was rushing around with his head high. Anytime she would ask him to slow up with the reins he would fling his hard as if to try to throw the bridle off. After about twenty minutes of trying to settle him she gave up and got off. The group voiced appropriately consoling words as I passed by to continue on with my duties.

A few days later, I bumped into Beth-Anne and asked her how Dipper was going.

"Not so good. I took him out for a ride down the laneway yesterday and he tried to buck me off."

I asked her how.

"Well, he was jig jogging the whole way as soon as I got on him. As we got past the paddock on the corner the horses in there ran up the fence line and he tried to take off. I pulled on the reins to stop him and that's when he put in an almighty buck. Luckily it was just one because I don't think I could have stayed on if he had put in a second. I don't know what's wrong with him, but he has been a real pain the last few days. I think it must be all the spring grass. He is just so stirred up when I take him out of his paddock."

This gave me something to think about. I didn't know anything about spring grass. I was curious to know what was so special about the grass at this time of year that caused horses to go crazy. I asked the boss about "spring grass".

"All the horses gets stirred up when the grass starts growing after winter. Something to do with the sugar or something in it. I dunno really. But ya just need to work them more often and harder and they get over it."

I took this explanation as fairly plausible. Something in the grass was causing changes in the horse's brains, which then made them go loco. It sounded to me like this spring grass was dangerous and maybe horses should be taken off paddocks and hand fed until the grass became safe again. Now that I was aware of the danger of spring grass, I started to notice other horses also acting a little crazy at times. Not always, but sometimes even the old plodding school horses had a little more zip in their movement than normal.

FERRET GRASS

A few days later I saw that Walt and Amos were coming back from a ride up to the quarry. We greeted each other in the usual way. I asked how their ride went and Walt replied that it was a sweet picnic.

"Did you have any trouble with the trucks by the quarry?" I asked.

"Nah matey, the horses were real steady and the trucks didn't bother 'em at all."

"So Walt, is the spring grass not bothering your horses?"

"No matey, they love it. Why would it?"

"Well, Beth-Anne reckons her horse is a little nuts because the grass is making him all hyper. And I see that lots of the boarders are having the same trouble. Even a couple of the school horses are acting differently."

"Well, that might be matey. But it probably ain't the grass that is the problem."

"Then what is, Walt?"

"Me dad use to call grass in the spring time, ferret grass, matey."

"Ferret grass! Why ferret grass?"

"Well matey, ferrets run around finding holes in things. Then they dive down into them holes and stir up trouble with whatever is in them holes – rabbits, snakes, echidnas, even wombats. That's what ferret grass does. Ya horse eats it and it finds holes in his trainin and his partnership with people and when it finds a hole it stirs up a whole lot of trouble."

"I think you have sort of lost me, Walt," I said.

"When the bluebirds of happiness bathe in the sunshine and peace reigns throughout the kingdom, most people can get along with their horse without too much trouble. But when ya horse starts eatin ferret grass, it gives him a whole lot more energy and his mind starts to thinkin about things other than goin along with the human. The rider says to walk, but the ferret grass makes the horse's mind think about goin faster. The rider says ride away from ya mates, but the ferret grass says to the horse go back to ya mates. It's a battle between what the rider tells the horse and what the ferret grass tells the horse. Sometimes, the ferret grass wins because the trainin and relationship with the rider is not as strong as the effect of the ferret grass. The ferret grass finds the holes in the trainin and exploits it."

"So Walt are you saying that the only way to overcome the effect of spring grass is better training?"

"A lot of the time, matey. The spring grass tells ya how strong is your relationship and where the holes are. As ya trainin gets better, the effect of the ferret grass gets less. Ya don't see me horse Burner bouncing off the walls do ya? He don't have to be lunged for half an hour every spring before I get on him. But a horse that might be in the earlier stages of his education might suffer the effects of ferretitus grassiosis."

I was to find over the years that Walt was absolutely right. Unwanted behaviour that coincides with spring grass is often just a sign that the training has not yet progressed to the stage we need it to be. Experience has taught me that this is often true with the effects of oestrus cycles in mares or handling stallions or horses on too much grain or lucerne. It's true that these factors can alter the way a horse behaves, but it is also true that when the training is up to scratch and the human and horse are a unit, that these factors don't really make much impact. I see this even with my own horses. I've owned a couple of mares that would behave like they needed an exorcism during spring in the early stages of training. But as the relationship between us grew stronger the effects of spring grass and hormones seem to dissolve to such an extent that they were forgotten.

But there is a caveat to all this. There is no doubt that horses can have allergies to feeds, and mares and colts can have hormonal dysfunctions. It is not very common, but occasionally behaviour relating to spring grass or weeds or reproductive function is not a training issue, but can be a physiological problem. Even though the majority of problems are training issues, you should not totally discount the possibility that some behaviour has an organic base.

IT'S NOT EASY BEING GREEN

His name was Prince William, but his paddock name was Willy. He was a rangy 16.2hh honey bay thoroughbred that Walt had broken in for a fellow called Lyle. Lyle was known to collect reject horses and then give them to anybody who wanted a horse. He didn't ride or even handle horses himself, but he liked having horses and playing Robin Hood. He had contacts everywhere and if you were talking to Lyle in the street or at a show it always took twice as long as necessary because Lyle had to say g'day and shake hands with everybody who passed by. Everybody knew Lyle and liked him but nobody knew what he did or where his money came from. Walt once told me that Lyle was brought up in a wealthy grazing family in the northern tablelands of NSW and had done everything in life a man could do except have a job.

Willy had been ridden for about 9 months before I got involved. Walt had done all the breaking in and after that the horse was given to a girl as a trail horse and for pony club. However, the girl's family had moved away and couldn't take Willy. Lyle was left looking for another home for Willy. In the meantime, Walt and Lyle asked me if I would do some work with the horse to keep him ticking over to make it easier to find a new home.

When I first started riding him he seemed quite nervous and unsure of what was being asked. I figured he was still very green because he had only been started a few months previously and then ridden by a kid. It was easy to see why he was so insecure and carried the anxiety he did. Everything about him was just like a baby getting started. He was terribly crooked – either dropping his shoulder or falling out on his turns. He threw his head up when told to go forward and leaned on the reins when asked to stop or backup. He even rubbernecked sometimes so that he would turn his head one way while moving in the opposite direction. I could see there was a lot of work ahead of me to get him right.

With all the worry he carried and the degree of greenness he exhibited I decided it was probably better to give him the benefit of the doubt for a while and just accept a try. I would ask something of him and when he gave it a thought I would release even before he followed through. I was sure that this was the right approach if I was to get Willy feeling better. After all, Walt and Amos had been telling me for a long time that I should always accept the smallest try when a horse is struggling.

"No point in goin for gold when the best a horse has got to give is chalk," Walt would say. "Chalk might be good enough for now."

So it was a chalk performance that I was looking for.

I can't say that Willy was a bad horse to handle or ride. He did everything I asked of him. But he wasn't a fun horse either. It appeared to me that he maintained an underlying level of worry, which got in the way of him being able to smoothly go from doing one thing to doing something else. For example, if I asked him to turn left, he would turn his nose to the left, drift his shoulder a little to the outside of the turn for two or three steps, then soften to the inside rein and bring his shoulder back to the direction I was asking and give me a really nice left turn. But then if I asked for a right turn we would have to go through the whole process again going to the right. It would happen every time. Ask Willy to do one thing and it would be a few steps before he would get it okay, but then ask for something else and it would take a few moments to do that right, then onto something else and again a few steps of correction were needed before that was good. It didn't matter what it was – right turn, left turn transitions; stop, go transitions; change of gait transitions. Even on the trail he always baulked at the first puddle that needed to be crossed. But once the first one was done, there was hardly ever a problem with any other puddles or drains, embankments or bridges for the rest of the ride.

However, the next ride was always the same – stop at the first so-called scary thing and once that was out of the way the rest was easy.

It was not much different when it came to the groundwork either. Every time I put a halter on Willy and lead him, he was draggy and needed to be towed for a few steps before coming with me under his own steam. Then he would be good for a while before he would forget all about the leading and start dragging behind again. It didn't matter what it was – hindquarter yields, forehand yields, backing up, lateral work, round yard liberty training etc. He always had to be reminded over and over again what it was to be soft and responsive because he could never hold that idea for very long.

"Matey, I got a call from Lyle last night. He thinks he might have a fella interested in the thoroughbred. How's he bin goin?" Amos stood at the stable door watching me shovel last night's manure into the barrow.

"Okay, I guess," I replied.

"What d'ya mean? Is he ready to show somebody or ain't he?"

"Yeah, I guess. Well I mean he's not as good as he could be, but he is better than most. He's safe, but unsure. He always needs a moment or two before he gives a try. It's like his brains fires a little slower than other horses and when I ask him to do something he needs time to come around to changing his resistance. "

"What d'ya mean, matey," Amos asked?

"Well, I dunno. It's like if you and Walt were reading something and you read fast and Walt reads slow. You would constantly be waiting for Walt to get to the end of the page so you could turn to the next page. That's what Willy is like. I'm constantly waiting for him to get to the conclusion of everything I ask him to do. I have to wait and wait before he softens and I can then ask for the next thing. Does that make sense?"

"Okay. Well listen, if ya got time tomorrow mornin I'll meet ya in the arena after ya done feedin. Have Willy saddled and ready to go and let's see if I can see somethin that might help. Ya know Walt broke that horse in and I don't reckon he would have left such a big trouble spot inside of him. So if somebody else has put it there, I reckon we can take it out again."

It was a beautiful day. The warmest and sunniest we had had in almost two months. I fed Willy first so that by the time I had finished feeding the rest he was done with breakfast and ready for saddling.

By the time Willy and I got to the arena, Amos and Walt were both sitting on the fence, waiting. I nodded to the old brothers. I felt a little under the gun with Walt watching.

As I came through the gate Amos spoke "just get ya self organized and ride around and we'll watch for a bit."

I hopped on Willy and ask him to walk. He started forward with not much energy, so I began to bump him with my legs to get some more life in his feet. This caused him to pick up speed as we headed up the long side. I decided to do a couple of hindquarter yields and check in to see where his mind was. I picked up the inside rein and brought it back to my belly button. At first Willy used this as an excuse to rest his head against the outside ring of the bit and he was quite heavy. He tilted his nose rather then flexed his neck muscles. He kept leaning forward on the inside rein which caused his shoulder to step to the outside of the turn and to push forward with his hindquarters when he should have been reaching across with his inside hind and shifting his weight off of his forehand. After about five or six steps he got a little lighter in my hand and a little less pushing forward, so I released the rein and allowed him to walk on.

"Now matey, do that agin on the other rein would y?" Amos shouted.

I repeated my attempt at a soft hindquarter yield on the opposite rein. But Willy didn't seem to feel there was a difference because the result was almost identical. He leaned on the rein and push forward through his outside shoulder until after a few tries he got a little softer and I released the rein again.

"Okay matey, can ya show us a back up?"

I started to take a feel of the reins and when Willy felt this was another thing he could lean on again. I kept taking up the feel more and more until he began to shift his weight back and took a step. I released. I tried again and this time Willy didn't lean quite so hard on the reins. It was an improvement so I released again. I repeated the back up a few more times and each time Willy's response was softer and less delayed.

"Walk him forward and do it again, matey"

I did as Amos asked. When I asked Willy to walk he was slow to respond and sluggish. After a few steps I picked up the feel of the reins and asked for a back up. He was once again heavy in my hand and when he stepped back he dragged his feet along the ground. I kept repeating the exercise until he was more on my page.

"Okay matey, come over here and let me have a ride," Amos commanded.

Walt said nothing as I dismounted. Amos took the reins and lined Willy up along side where he was sitting on the fence so the frail old man could mount this 16.2 giant. As Amos put a feel on the reins to bring the horse closer to the fence Willy leaned back. The next instant Amos slapped the fence with a lead rope he held in his other hand. The *'thwack'* sound made Willy leap sideways. Amos asked again and the horse sidled up to him. Amos mounted, adjusted the stirrups and rode off. After he got a little distance from Walt and me he turned the horse around so they were facing us.

"Okay matey, I'm goin to ask Willy to walk off."

Thud! Amos' legs crashed in on Willy's ribs. The horse leaped forward and trotted off at high speed. Amos circled around back to the spot where he first asked for the walk and stopped Willy.

"I'll ask again."

I couldn't see what Amos did, but Willy walked off with a purpose. He seemed to be going with the notion he had some place to be.

Amos picked up the left rein and I could see he was going to ask for a hindquarter yield. The look in Willy's eye and the way he began to set his body up told me that he was preparing to lean and drift out through his shoulder. But at that moment Amos reefed the left rein so firmly that Willy's stumbled off balance. Even though he didn't quite step his inside hind leg under his body he didn't push forward either. Amos released the reins and asked again. This time when Willy started to lean and Amos started to firm up on the left rein Willy shifted his weight onto his hind end and looked around to the left. Amos released the reins again and sat quietly while rubbing Willy on the neck. He asked Willy to walk off and this time I observed Amos adjust the angle of his pelvis. Willy walked forward like he was marching. The rest of the ride was similar. Amos would ask something of Willy and if he was late or braced against the aid, Amos stopped asking and began demanding.

D'ya get it matey?" Walt asked.

"I'm a little confused Walt. I thought I was suppose to reward the smallest try, but Amos is pretty demanding of Willy that he get it right and not just try to get it right," I replied.

"Not at all. Amos is acceptin the smallest try. The difference is what ya think is a try and what Amos thinks is a try are two different things. The way ya workin Willy is the way ya might work a horse the first time or two he is learnin a job. But how many times ya think Willy has had to walk when asked or stop when asked or a hindquarter yield? This ain't his first time and he knows what is bein asked. He has had enough ridin to know these things, but ya treatin him like it's his first time. Ya teachin him to not try any harder than he tried when I first started playin with him. It's time he started wearin long pants and became a real horse with a real job that's important to him. What was a try for Willy last year ain't a try any more. He ain't no longer putting in the effort. He's just pretendin to go through the motions. He's doin it in his sleep.

"When I started Willy I gave him plenty of time to figure out what it was to try and give a hindquarter yield or to back up. He got pretty good at it too. He would feel me start to ask and he'd prepare. But the importance of it has lost it's meanin for him 'cause between you and the girl that had him before, he's lost his try. The try he had last year shouldn't be the same try he has today. If he ain't able to do better it's because ya still treatin him like he's too green. As a horse gets better and learns the meanin of ya reins or ya legs or both, ya gotta ask and expect more from ya horse. Otherwise, he will spend the rest of his life being green. All Amos is doin is tellin Willy that he knows that Willy knows and he ain't beggin him. Amos asks Willy very politely, then he stops beggin and tells him he better listen when Amos speaks."

I think a lot of people are guilty of keeping their horse green because what they accept as a try or change today is the same thing they accepted a hundred rides ago. I guess psychologist would call some riders *enablers* because by their behaviour they can enable a horse with ten years experience to still behave like a green horse. Our expectations of our horses should progress as our horses progress. We still need to be mindful of what they can and can't do and what is fair and what is unfair. But we don't want to be the ones holding them back because we continue to treat them as greener than they really are.

MOTIVATION TO SEARCH

When I think back over some of the horses I have trained for other people many of them blend into each other. But a few stand out. Mainly because I think they triggered a leap in my understanding. One of those horses was Orpheus. He was a stout Andalusian cross gelding that stood about 15.1 and had a jet black coat and no white anywhere. He was beautiful.

I was asked to break in Orpheus when I was in my late teens and just finishing high school. I hadn't had much experience with horses of Spanish blood and was really looking forward to it. His owner told me he was super quiet and had been handled by his breeder since birth. The owner told me that when she was looking at Orpheus the breeder hopped on him bareback and bridleless and walked him around a yard. It was a first time for Orpheus and he didn't seem to care at all. That was the selling point for her.

When I began working with Orpheus the thing that was soon very obvious was how unresponsive he was. He led about as well as Walt's old Ford truck would lead. I tried swinging the lead rope and I tried driving him with a flag and I tried using a whip. He would make an initial leap forward off the lead rope then go back to dragging along. I repeated and repeated until my arms were ready to fall off. Every time I got stronger with the flag or whip he would come forward for that moment, but then he would instantly quit when I stopped using them. I started to think to myself "didn't he know that I was going to use the flag again if he quit?" I was beginning to wonder if Orpheus didn't care about pressure or was just too stupid to know how to respond to it.

After a few days I saddled him and tried to get him to move around the round pen. Again, I didn't get much response. He didn't buck with the saddle, which I liked. But he also hardly moved when I asked him to walk, trot or canter in the round pen, which I didn't like. I didn't know what I was going to do to get this guy to make a change that was going to last for more than a few seconds.

"Well matey, I don't think he is stupid," said Walt when I went to ask him about Orpheus. "The difference between a smart horse and one that we think ain't smart is how quick they learn. And learnin is dependent on how much a horse searches for an answer. So it ain't about how intelligent he is, but how much he cares about searchin for a way out of the pressure."

"Walt, are you saying that Orpheus is smart, but he just doesn't care?" I asked.

"No matey, I'm saying I don't know how smart he is, but it don't make much difference because he is smart enough to be as smart as a horse needs to be to be a smart horse!"

""Uh?" I said in my wondering what the hell Walt just said.

"And he does care about things. He just don't care about you are doin with him. Ya ain't found a way to motivate him enough to search for a way out of the pressure ya put on him," Walt continued.

Walt suggested we try an experiment. We moved Orpheus to a paddock that he would have to share with a sweet chestnut mare called Mary. The moment we let Orpheus off the halter he trotted up to Mary wide eyed and keen to make friends. As soon as they sniffed shoulders Mary turned her heels to Orpheus and kicked him with both back feet. She kept kicking at him as she ran at him, hind end first. Orpheus scampered for his life. Walt said Orpheus would be alright and we should leave them to sort it out and check on them tomorrow.

The next day we went to check on them and they were grazing almost side by side. But when Mary wanted Orpheus to move she just gave him a look and he gave her space. The rest of the time Orpheus followed her around like they were Velcro.

MOTIVATION TO SEARCH

"See matey how Mary inspired the stubbornness out that black geldin. One look from her is all the motivation he needs to move them feet. How much flagin and hollerin did ya have to do to get him to move like that?"

"I get your point, Walt. But I don't know how much more I can do. Orpheus just seems to have a pretty low opinion of anything I do."

"Well matey, it ain't all your fault. A lot of them imprinted horses are taught that the person ain't worth listenin to. They're taught from babies to pay no attention to people. So you was battlin against four years of bad handlin. Tomorrow I'll give ya a hand with gettin old Orpheus there to start thinkin about searchin for answers. We'll start with comin forward off the lead rope."

The next day Walt met me in the jump paddock. I had Orpheus in hand and he was in the cab of his Ford truck. Walt got out with a long rope and tied it to the halter. He wrapped the lead rope around the rear bumper of the truck and handed me the tail end. I sat on the back tray while Walt got back into the cab. Walt slowly drove forward and when I shouted that Orpheus was leaning on the rope he smoothly but quickly accelerated until Orpheus trotted with slack in the rope. Walt slowed down to a stop and we repeated the process. It took about 20 repetitions before Orpheus stopped leaning on the rope as soon as the truck rolled forward. It took another 10 repetitions for Orpheus to learn the halt to trot transition and another 10 or so to be clear about trot to canter. Over the coming days we repeated the leading off the truck and then graduated to leading off another horse and then leading by a person from foot.

From there Walt helped me with round pen work, hindquarter disengagements, forehand yields and lariat work. With each new challenge Orpheus became more focused and more involved in what was being asked. In the process Orpheus sometimes became quite worried about things what was being asked. I talked to Walt about it.

"That's a good thing, matey. He ain't shuttin you out like he did and he is startin to care. When he cares about you he will care about pressure. When he cares about pressure he will search harder for a way out of the pressure. He ain't stayin bothered when he finds what he was searchin for, so he is learnin a better way to respond instead of repeatin the same pattern over and over again of pushin against any pressure."

I saw that Orpheus would get worried when he tried to respond but couldn't find the answer. And it occurred to me that he was now behaving like a normal horse. Walt had helped get this horse to behave and respond like just like lots of other horses I had seen. It was like he had knocked down a wall that the real Orpheus was hiding behind and now Orpheus could express his real feelings that had always been there but had remained deep inside and hidden from the world. I asked Walt some more about teaching a horse to search.

"A horse that is motivated to search for the answer looks to us to be more intelligent and more trainable. But we can train the search out of a horse by criticizin everythin he does or by tryin to control everythin he does – like in that foal imprint thing. You can discourage a response in an encouragin way to build a search or in a discouragin way to kill the search. It's all up to us."

Orpheus remains an important horse in my life because of what he and Walt taught me about teaching a horse to search. There were other horses that were just as important and I'm sure there are others in my future will have even more important lessons for me to learn. But I miss those times when Walt and Amos were there to guide me. Now that they are gone and no longer around to help me with answers I realize how lucky I am that they trained me to search too.

WHAT IS A TRICK?

Not too long ago I heard a very experienced dressage rider and judge giving an ear bashing to her friend about what happened at a horsemanship clinic that she had recently attended. She had said that it wasn't normally her thing to go to that type of trainer anyway, but she had heard about him and was curious enough to watch for a day. She said she knew it was a mistake when she saw all those horses being ridden around without ever asking for a contact and having to do hindquarter disengagement which for her was the antithesis of what riding should be about. But the final straw was when the clinician did a demonstration on how to teach a horse to bow. For the lady doing the talking this was the ultimate indignity for a horse. Her view was that nothing showed more disrespect for a horse than to have them perform tricks for the amusement of people.

This was not the first time I had heard this notion voiced. When I was a kid, Walt and Amos were always playing around with teaching tricks to horses. I remember one Sunday when the owner of the riding school had agreed to have a busload of kids from the local centre visit and pat horses. Walt offered to entertain the kids with a few tricks. I particularly remember Walt fumbling around with trying to saddle his horse Banger and fussing with putting the saddle pad on straight. As he turned away to pick up the saddle, Banger would reach around, grab the corner of the pad in his teeth and tear it off his back. Walt then turned back to his horse ready to swing the saddle on and see the pad lying on the ground where Bangar had dropped it. Walt then put the saddle down in frustration and dust off the saddle pad and place it back on Banger. Banger would stand quietly without shifting, but as soon as Walt's back was turned to get the saddle again Banger would whisk that pad off and throw it away. Walt would pretend he didn't know what was happening and start again with his most frustrated expression. This time as he turned to collect the saddle, he would quickly swing back to stare at Banger who would be standing quietly and not even look at Walt. Walt would spin back to look at Banger two or three times as he went for the saddle, but Banger was just not moving. Then as Walt bent to pick up the saddle, around would come Banger's teeth and throw that pad in the air to land four or five feet away. This would have the kids howling with laughter. Then Walt put his saddle back on the ground, picked up the pad and put it on Banger's back again. He kept one hand on the pad as he tried to stretch for the saddle with his other hand. Of course, Walt made sure the saddle was out of reach. Walt would stretch and stretch until it was obvious that he had to let go of the saddle pad if he was going to pick up the saddle. Just as he took his hand off Banger's back, Banger whipped around and pulled the pad off his back, dropped it on the ground and then stood on it with his left foreleg. Now Walt pretended to be really mad and the kids were laughing so hard at him. He tried to pull the pad from under Banger's hoof, but that didn't work. He then heaved and pulled to get Banger to lift his leg, but that didn't work either. Walt was hopping mad now and threw his hat on the ground and said all sorts of naughty things about his horse. Finally, one of the kids (about ten years old) that boarded her horse at the riding school picked up Banger's foot, put the saddle pad on Banger's back and then picked up the saddle and finished saddling Walt's horse. Those kids from the centre thought that was the funniest thing they had ever seen and Banger was the world's smartest horse.

While I was watching the performance of Walt and Banger I stood near a couple of the teachers from the centre. Towards the end of the show I over heard one teacher say to the other, "Look at that poor horse. He is such a nice fellow, but those tricks are so undignified. I don't like it when horses get treated like toys."

WHAT IS A TRICK?

This statement took me aback somewhat because I knew Walt would be the last person on earth to treat a horse without respect. In fact, he often had more respect for horses than he did for most humans. It made me wonder why the teacher would think such a thing. And it occurred to me a little later that people equate teaching tricks with circus training or caged animals. They often associate trick training of an animal with bears tethered on chains or lions housed in cages little bigger than an office desk.

At the end of the day, when the kids and teachers had gone I went in search of Walt. "Walt what's the difference between a trick and a training exercise?" I asked.

"What d'ya mean, matey?"

"Well, I heard one of the teachers say that she thought Bangar was being treated without respect because he was being used to make people laugh at him. She said that the tricks are undignified."

"I dunno, matey. I thought the kids were laughin at Bangar makin me look silly. Maybe it was Bangar that was direspectin me.

"I guess that's true. He did make you look pretty dumb," I had to agree.

"I know what the teacher was sayin, though. Tricks can be disrespectful. But they don't have to be," Walt added.

"What do you mean?"

"Well matey, the thing that I think is undignified is workin with a horse in a way that ya don't give a hoot about how he feels about the work. I think treatin him like an object whose only purpose is to entertain people is disrespectful of the horse. They have feelins and needs and if ya don't care about them that's exploitation. And in my book exploitin a horse is undignified."

"But what about the difference between teaching him to bow and teaching him to jump a fence or do a collected canter? Do you think one is a trick and one is legitimate work?" I asked.

"Not to the horse. He don't see one as worthy of his esteemed position in life and the other as demeanin to his status. To a horse it's all the same. There ain't any more merit in a horse bowing than a horse winning a dressage competition. It's only people who rank these things as bein respectable or not. Horses don't see any difference. It's all work to him."

"So why do we call one type of work "tricks" and the other type exercises?" I had to ask.

"I dunno matey. I guess people like to categorize things. For me, I see that anythin that is taught to a horse that he don't feel okay about is a trick. He does what we ask, but if ain't got his mind and heart invested in it it seems like a trick to me. It don't matter if it's loadin onto a truck or doin a flying change. If he's only doin it 'cause he has to, it feels like a trick to me."

Walt had given me a lot to think about. I started to watch other horses with a new set of eyes. Even the horse's I was riding had me thinking about whether I was doing quality work or just teaching them tricks. It's not always easy to be sure because sometimes poor quality training can look like good quality training. Sometimes the highest level of exercise can be a trick and the most basic trick can be the highest quality of training. But I believe horses know the difference even if we don't.

CAN A HORSE ENJOY WORK?

This is a question I have often pondered. Every time somebody tells me that their horse loves to work, he loves to jump, he loves to event, he loves to chase cows, he loves to go out on a trail ride, I ask myself does he really love it or is the owner confusing what a horse is doing with what he is feeling?

I had the chance to work a horse for one of the neighbours of the riding school. The horse's name was Tucker and he was a big strong Percheron/Arab gelding. Tucker was only 4 years old and had only been broken in. He was coming home from the breaker and the owners wanted me to take his training a little further. I was there when he arrived. He came off the truck prancing. Fire was coming out of his nostrils and his tail more than adequately told the story of his Arabian ancestry. He was led to a pretty large paddock with about fifteen head of dry cows. It was obvious from the get go that Tucker had never seen cows before and the sight of them stopped his heart in mid beat. He was convinced he was going to die if he didn't run for his life. Luckily, it was such a large paddock that Tucker could get quite a distance from the cows without having to annihilate any fencing. In his mind, being at the opposite end of the pasture was sufficient to keep his relationship with his bovine housemates amicable.

Over the next few days I visited Tucker regularly to check on him, but other than that I was happy to just let him settle in. Walt and Amos visited at my request and they said all the appropriate things about what a nice horse he was and how he would be a good project for me. After about a week I began to ease him into work. We started in the round yard and I discovered one or two holes in his training that I wanted to fix before riding him out on trails. But within a week Tucker and I were out and about. He was a quick learner and lots of fun to ride.

One day about three weeks after Tucker had arrived, I went over to catch him for a session and I noticed he was following the cows. I stood and watched for a time. Tucker began chasing the mob of cows. At first I thought he was just madly chasing them, but he wasn't at all. He ran the herd down to the far end of the paddock, around some trees, up the opposite side and back into the corner from where they had come. He then selected one cow and cut her from the herd. He ran her down the paddock, around the trees and back to the herd. He even turned her when she tried to go around the trees in the wrong direction. When the first cow got back to the herd, Tucker cut out another one and did the same. He pinned his ears and stretched his neck out to move her along at a lively pace when she showed some hesitancy to get her feet moving. I watched totally fascinated. I had never before seen a horse work cows by himself. Tucker was working and by all accounts he was having fun. I figured there was a bit of cow horse in this young Percheron/Arab.

I told Amos about it and he said it didn't surprise him at all. He reckoned that once Tucker figured out he could move those cows he'd stop being afraid of them and start teaching them who was boss in that paddock.

I stopped riding Tucker regularly a short time after that. The owner figured I had got him to a good spot and he'd take it from there. But I did get to ride him one more time. A few weeks later the neighbour asked me if I would help him move some cows. He said I could ride Tucker and he would ride his old mare. I jumped at the chance because I remembered that Tucker loved to chase cows.

We rode out to the paddock to gather the mob and bring them through the gate. I directed Tucker to go around the left flank of the herd and come up behind. He kept trying to swing around to get to the front, but I managed to keep things steady. At the back he got a little on his toes. He shook his head and when I tried to push him onto a cow that was dawdling at the back he refused to get near her. When she turned to look at him he nearly leaped out of his skin. I was doing everything I could to keep him from leaving. In the end I had to get off because he was unsettling the cows too much. I led him on foot and herded the cows to the neighbour's yard. I was more than a little perplexed by Tucker's behaviour. I knew he wasn't afraid of the cows any more and even seem to enjoy chasing them. So why was he behaving like a total pill?

Apparently, the tale of my prowess as a stockman was worthy news for the grapevine. The next day everybody at the riding school had heard about my embarrassment. Just a few weeks earlier I had been boasting about what a great horse Tucker was and how he was a natural cow horse. Now I had egg all over my face.

I guessed that Walt had probably heard about what had happened and my guess was confirmed when he greeted me with, "how's it goin, Clancy?" Which I presumed was some comical reference to the poem "The Man From Snowy River."

"Hi Walt. It didn't take long for you to hear what happened," I said.

"Don't worry too much, matey. It's all new to him. He'll figure his job out."

"But Walt, I thought he would really like moving cows and wasn't scared of them anymore. I told you about Tucker chasing them around those trees. He seemed to be having a ball doing that. I don't understand why he got so upset yesterday."

"Well, matey when Tucker was chasing them cows in his paddock it was his idea – nobody else's just his. Yesterday it was your idea – not his. He probably wasn't so much bothered by the cows as he was by doing it your way. Ya see, when a horse has an idea to do somethin it doesn't cause him any trouble to do it – me might even enjoy doin it. But when a person tries to make the horse have an idea, then doin things that way can cause him some concern."

"Well then Walt, are you saying that even things a horse enjoys can be hard when the human gets involved?" I asked.

"It happens all the time, matey."

"So do you think a horse can ever enjoy working?" was my next question.

"Well matey, I don't really know for sure. Does a horse ever know happiness? I think that's a question only a horse can answer. But what I do reckon is that a horse can feel okay with workin. I figure if the trainin is right then a horse ain't bothered by what a rider might ask him to do. But ya don't see too many horse's that ain't bothered."

"What about those horses you see hooning around the jumping course? Don't they like to jump?" I asked

"Matey, most of them are runnin for their lives. They are just tryin to get the job done as fast and easily as they know how. But they don't feel okay inside. They're more bothered than you or I can ever know. If they were really lovin it, don't ya think they'd be lookin for somethin to jump all day long? Here's a test for ya. Get one of them horses that love to jump, put him in an arena with a jump in the middle. Put a rider on him and have no bridle on the horse. Ask the rider to ride the horse forward, but to use nothin to direct the horse where to go – just ask him to go. How many of them horses that love to jump do ya reckin would choose to go over that jump?"

"So, are you saying that horses don't like to work?"

"No matey, I ain't saying that. What I believe is that for most of us the best we can hope for is to have a horse feel okay or not bothered about being ridden. I'm pretty happy if my horse don't get worried about doin a job. Most of us don't ever get our horses to feelin okay. There are plenty of horses out there that get pretty stressed even about the little things like bein caught or have a saddle fitted. There are more horses than ya can count that if given the choice wouldn't spend one second of their time around humans."

"But Walt, if that's true why do they let themselves be caught? Some even come over to be caught," I queried.

"Horses can learn that being caught is their job. They just learn to do a job whether they like it or not. Look at what happen with Tucker. He's not worried about the cows. When given the chance he found he had a fine time chasin them cows. But then ya got in the picture and turned it into a job. Why did that happen? It happened because he don't feel ok inside about being told to work. He feels good about movin cows, but not in takin orders from the human. Tucker is a good example of a horse that is polite and obedient, but he don't feel real happy about the human or doin what he is told. He does things ya tell him, but he don't feel good about it. Most horses are the same. When ya've got a horse workin for ya and he ain't bothered by it – whether or not he's happy about it – but he ain't bothered by it - then ya've got somethin most everyone else is still looking for."

I knew then that in his own way Walt was telling me that despite the progress I had made with Tucker there were still unresolved trouble inside him about working with people. Trouble spots I didn't know existed were brought to the surface during my attempts to show the world that Tucker was a natural cow horse. A cloud of despondency fell over me for the poor job I had done. I promised myself that it would be the last time I worked with a horse without considering what the horse was getting out of it.

FOOD, GLORIOUS FOOD

I learned a secret. A pony called Whistler taught the secret to me. He was a 10-year-old Shetland ridden by a 9-year-old girl called Amber. Whistler showed me how to solve world hunger. It came to me like a flash when I was watching a news report on television about the starving people of northern India. The solution to fixing it so that nobody ever starved again was to study how Whistler turned 1kg of feed into 20 kg of fat. If we could harness Whistler's secret and use it for people then nobody would go hungry again.

I had never seen a horse so food oriented as Whistler. Amos used to say that Whistler would sell his mother for a blade of grass and then chuckle to himself at having made a joke about Whistler's mother (fortunately I was too young to be in on the joke that Whistler's mother was the subject of a famous painting).

Amber found that she could get Whistler to do most things when enticed with the promise of food. He used to be a pill to catch, but when Amber started bringing carrots with her to the paddock Whistler soon learned to meet her at the gate and slip his nose into the halter. Loading into a float, tying up, saddling, standing still for the farrier were all problems that were taken care of with a little cunning use of food rewards.

I hadn't ever given much thought to Amber and Whistler until one day at the Royal Show I had a discussion with Walt and Amos.

I had qualified in the C grade showjumping with Hank who was owned by a friend. Walt and Amos came along to help me get ready for my classes, but also to visit the livestock and the cakes and preserve pavilions. They loved the cakes and sweets. During a lull in the competition I wandered around with the old brothers to look for somewhere to have lunch. We came across a small portable yard with a couple of people inside with a horse and a horse float and a crowd of about 30 people watching from outside. Apparently, it was demonstration on how to load a horse onto a float.

The fellow in the yard asked the lady who owned the horse to show people what he was like to load onto the float. She proceeded to lead the horse towards the ramp, but just as he got there he ducked to the side and missed the ramp. The owner brought him back and he did it again. Then when she brought him to the ramp the third time he stopped, leaned on the lead rope and ran backwards until he got to the other side of the yard. The lady said that this was typical except sometimes he would rear and strike if she got more forceful with him. The fellow thanked her and took the lead rope.

He said he would teach the horse to load quietly by giving him positive reward only. He talked about fear and claustrophobia, gentleness and calmness etc. before starting with the training. The fellow produced a toy clicker that made a clicking noise when it was pressed. They were often found in the Cadbury and liquorice show bags. He explained how by asking the horse to do something, then releasing while pressing the clicker and then follow with a food treat the horse would learn what to do and at the same time have only a positive experience. This was the first time I had heard of clicker training and I later learned that it was how the US Navy had trained dolphins.

The trainer asked the horse to approach the ramp of the float. At the first step forward he released and at the same time clicked. He then gave the horse a sugar cube. Then another step, release/click and a sugar cube. When the horse got to the ramp he baulked. The trainer waited, but the instant the horse leaned forward he released, clicked and gave him another sugar cube. Pretty soon the horse was able to go into the float one step at a time with the trainer rewarding him for every step. The horse was then backed out and the process was repeated.

FOOD, GLORIOUS FOOD

On the third time the trainer didn't reward for each step forward, but instead kept asking until the horse took two steps. Then he released, clicked and treated. You could see the horse searching for the treat. When the trainer didn't reward him after just one step the horse started to search the trainer for the sugar. Eventually, he gave up searching and tried another step for which he was rewarded. With more repetition the trainer withheld the click and reward until the horse made more of an effort. After about 45 minutes the horse was going in and out of the float quite eagerly and only being rewarded when he went all the way in and then all the way out.

I was pretty impressed at the change in the horse and thought that this was a technique that I should investigate a little further. Just as I was thinking this I heard a familiar croaky voice.

"Excuse me son, but I was wonderin about somethin. Now that ya got that horse to go in and out of the trailer, can ya get him to just go halfway in or halfway out and stop 'im?" Amos asked the trainer.

The fellow thought about it for a minute and it was obvious the answer was not immediately clear to him.

"I haven't been asked that before, but the method relies on a targeted purpose for the reward. The point of using clicker training is to give the horse a clear target that he must reach in order to get his food reward. In this case, I eventually made the target to be going into the float and coming out of the float. I guess if you change the target to be going only halfway in, then you'd have to re-train the horse for the new target. But I can't see why that would matter because why would you want you horse to only be halfway in a float? It'd look pretty silly going down the road like that."

There were a few laughs from the crowd.

"Thanks son," said Amos.

In the truck home that night I brought up the subject of the demonstration and asked Amos about his question.

"Matey, did ya notice how fixated that horse became on where the next lump of sugar was comin from? Once the horse figured out that if he did somethin he would get some sugar, he began lookin at what to do to get the sugar. He was pokin around that fellas pockets and mouthin his arm huntin for the sugar. When he didn't get sugar he got more fidgety and was tossin his head. After awhile he got the picture to take another step and the sugar would be comin his way, but if he didn't get it he got pretty bothered."

"But Amos, he did learn to go into the float and when he started he wouldn't even put a foot on the ramp," I said.

Walt piped in. "No matey, he didn't learn to go in the float. All he learned was how to push the right buttons in order to get the vendin machine with the sugar to pop one out. The horse's focus was on the food, not on listenin to the fella. If he was really listenin to that young bloke he'd have been able to stop him at any point with no trouble because he would be mentally connected to the human. But the fella only taught him what he needed to do to get a lump of sugar. The mental connection was to the sugar not the fella."

"So do you think it's bad to reward a horse with food as a training technique?" I asked.

"Matey, the food ain't the problem. It's how ya use it. Horses love to eat and food is a powerful motivator. Just look at how Amber has trained Whistler to be caught. She can't go into that paddock without that tub of lard on legs tryin to harass her. It ain't because he loves her, it's because he sees her as a mobile feed bin. It's the same when she ties him up for the farrier. If he didn't have a flake of hay in front of him how long d'ya think it would be before he started stompin and fussin for his food? It's pretty rare to see a person use food as a reward and have a strong connection to the horse that ain't about the food. I reckon people should stay away from usin food to train horses. For most people it is just substitutin one problem with another."

I see the problems of food reward on a regular basis. The mental fixation on food when a person is working with a horse so often gets in the way of real communication back and forth between horse and human. I want to be more important to my horse than a slice of carrot or a biscuit of hay.

STRAIGHT AS A VICAR IN A COFFIN

"Amos, how do I get this horse to be straight?" I asked.

"Well matey, whatever ya did to get him crooked, just reverse it," was the retort!

The horse in question was called Razor and had been given to me to educate by a very nice fellow called Ted. Ted had got Razor from his brother who had retired him from racing only 6 months earlier. Ted wanted Razor for pleasure and club level competition. Ted's wife was an already keen and accomplished horsewoman who had decided that Ted should join her in her favourite pursuit. As most husbands who stay married learn 'resistance is futile', so Ted's wife's interest became Ted's interest.

Razor had somehow become my project. Walt and Amos told Ted they didn't have time to help him and that I would be able to sort things out for Razor and Ted. I was not asked about this, but was told about it as Walt handed me the lead rope one sunny day a week after Razor had arrived.

Razor was a pretty straightforward horse for an off the track thoroughbred. Like most thoroughbreds he had an excellent mind and although racing had screwed him up a bit, it was not too difficult to tap into the good that lay beneath. I began with teaching him to lead well and to stay mentally tuned into me. He was easily distracted by anything that moved within the bounds of the southern hemisphere. As we progressed I got more particular about his distraction and he slowly began to focus with more earnest and a softness that you rarely see in an ex-race horse.

When it came to riding, Razor was a lot more reactive than I had anticipated. He started to leave in a panic as soon as I tried to mount. The change from marshmallow to monster happened so quickly I was not prepared. Luckily I didn't get my leg over and dropped back to the ground before being committed to the saddle. The next time I was more prepared and so was Razor. I spent quite sometime getting him ready for me to mount. When I did climb on board he stood still, but was a bubbling volcano inside ready to spill over anytime. I got off again, moved him half a circle and got on again. I repeated this about five times before asking him to move.

Instead of putting leg on him to move I simply asked him to turn from the left rein. This was enough to unbalance him and get him mobile. I didn't worry that his turn had no bend. I was just hoping to survive the ride. I kept turning him in wide sweeping circles left and right. He walked as if he was about to break through a sheet of ice on a frozen lake. The change from left to right rein caused him to shudder through his whole body and leap. It took at least one stride before finding the walk again. I sat as quietly as I could hoping not to trigger an explosion.

After a few minutes I jumped off and put Razor away. I was mad at myself because I left him in the same spot that we started. He was no better for having ridden him. The next day I told myself I was going to ride more positively and exorcise the trouble out of Razor. Which I did. He was better to ride from the start, but still a jumble of nerves. Nevertheless, I pushed him to listen to the reins and legs, but kept him on the right side of trouble. I kept taking him to the edge and back and each time he got more confident and less worried as we pushed the boundaries of his comfort.

Over the next several days, I rode Razor out of the round yard and all over the riding school. I figured he needed to be allowed to move and not necessarily be schooled in the arena. He spooked quite a bit when somebody would appear around a corner or the boss started up the tractor. But when it was over, it was over. I was beginning to really like this fellow. He wasn't as soft to ride as Walt's horse or as focused on me as Amos would have him, but overall he was doing great.

When I was happier with the way he was travelling around the property I decided it was time to school him in the arena. I worked on his circles and serpentines, his halts and rein back. They were okay, but the thing that was most clear to me was how crooked he travelled all the time. His hindquarters were always drifting to the inside – especially on the long side straight. It was acceptable at the walk, bad at the trot and almost lateral at the canter. And it was worse going to the left than the right. I tried fixing it by using more inside leg behind the girth, but this just made him go faster. I tried moving his shoulder more to the inside, but that only stiffened him even more.

After several days of riding in the arena most things were showing clear improvement, except his crookedness. I decide to talk to Amos about it.

"Well matey, whatever ya did to get him crooked, just reverse it!"

"But I didn't do anything to cause it, Amos."

"It's more likely to be what ya didn't do, matey," he said.

"Like what?"

"What causes crookedness, matey?"

"I dunno!"

"Matey, it's a resistance thing. Crookedness is when some part of a horse is workin harder than another part. Ya just have to figure out what part is bracin and what it's bracin to do and ya got it fixed."

I must have had the look on my face that said "What are you talking about old man?" because he went on.

"A horse is always tryin to do what he is thinkin. If Razor is goin up the long side and his backside is stickin in, it's because he is thinkin to be wantin to be goin to the outside. He is settin up his rear engine to push his front out to the outside 'cause that's where he is thinkin to be. Most times crookedness is a resistance. Sometimes it can be a physical problem like an injury, but most times it's a resistance to be goin the direction he's goin. If there was a bucket of grain at the end of the arena, he'd be as straight as a vicar in a coffin headin to that bucket, but as wayward as a slow movin creek goin away from the bucket."

"Well how do I get him straighter, Amos?" I asked.

"Ya change his thinkin. At the moment he ain't real good at lettin ya tell him where to take his mind. He needs practice at committin to thinkin where ya send him.

"Two things ya have to work on, matey. First ya gotta give Razor a purpose in where he's goin. He ain't thinkin out ahead of him with an effort. Whether ya ridin straight ahead or on a turn, a horse should always be ridin a line. His mind should be on that line. See that line ahead in ya mind and get him to see it too by ridin with an effort as if to fall off that line would get ya both killed. Not enough people put an effort to ride a line. They go to move their horse and the very first step the horse shifts his weight to the left or right – he ain't steppin straight. Get him between ya hands and ya legs the very first step as best ya can. It won't be very good at first and it will look like ya are ridin a drunken horse on a jumpin castle. But with practice he will learn to get between them reins and ya legs and be as straight as a light beam."

"What's the second thing I have to work on, Amos?"

"The second thing is to get him bendin. The best way I know how to straighten a horse is to bend him. At the moment he is stiff like a fence rail nailed in the middle to a post – if ya move one end, it moves the other end. Get him flexible and bendin so ya can adjust any part of him without upsettin the other parts. It will also help him think around curves."

"How?" I asked.

"Well matey, lots of circles and parts of circles. Lots of sideways too. Circles with him bendin right, then overbendin, then counter bendin. Get him so ya can put his shoulders on or off the track without shiftin his backside. Then change by puttin his bum on or off the track without movin his shoulders. But ALWAYS get a bend. And when ya do this ya want him to do it from the reins more than from ya legs. Most people try to move a horse by their legs and let the horse stay stiff and braced against the reins. Don't do that. Make sure ya reins can direct any part of his body without ya legs. Just use ya legs to keep the energy in his feet, but don't direct him with them. As he gets softer and between them reins, he will get straighter. Later when he is really good off them reins, ya can start askin to step off ya legs and seat – but not before ya can do it from ya reins only. Otherwise, he will stay stiff to the bend."

STRAIGHT AS A VICAR IN A COFFIN

I spent weeks practising what Amos had to teach me. He was a great help and even rode Razor for me a few times to clear up some of the confusion I had. I didn't know you could do lateral work with no legs until I saw Amos demonstrate shoulder in with out legs to direct the horse. It was an eye-opening education on how to help get a horse soft in his mind, through his body and straight. It is something I continue to practice today with horses. I know most people would never consider doing laterals with reins only and think it to be incorrect. But until I ride another horse as soft and straight as my own I don't think I will change my mind.

TRAINING MOZ

Going to auctions and buying horses for training and later selling them was a way for the old men to supplement their meagre income. It wasn't that Walt and Amos were exactly horse dealers. I mean they didn't have paddocks full of horses for anybody to buy who had cash in their pockets. They took in only a few horses in a year. They were discerning with what they bought and even more discerning to whom they sold. Horses were not a commodity to be turned over to make a quick dollar. Care went into their training and care went into choosing who bought them.

One day Walt and Amos came home from the sale yard with a paint gelding. They didn't know his name, but because of the pattern of his coat it was decided to call him Mosaic or Moz as I ended up calling him. Moz was about 5 years old and broken in. Not much was known about him, but the brothers thought he was a strong athletic type and would make a good all rounder for an adult rider or good pony club kid. He was eye catching enough that people would want him just for his colour, but Walt and Amos would make sure that he was going well enough that he would find a home with good horse people.

I didn't have much to do with Moz in the coming months, but would occasionally see Walt take him out on a trail ride or play with kneeling down or load him onto the old truck. In fact I never really thought much at all about Moz until one day Walt approached me about him.

"Matey, would ya like to work Mosaic for me as a project for a bit? I gone and bought them other two horses and I'm a bit stretched for time. Them other horses need a bit more workin with than the paint. Ya'd be doin me a favour if ya could keep the paint tickin over until me and Amos find a buyer."

"Ah, okay Walt. I guess so. I don't know how much time I can commit to riding him, but I should be able to do three or four times a week if that's okay?" I said.

"That'll be plenty, matey. He don't need a lot, but I don't want to find a buyer when he's been doin nothin but standin in the paddock for a month."

"What sort of work do you want me to give him? Is there anything special I need to be working on?" I asked.

"Nah matey. He just needs ridin. He's good on the trail if ya want to take him out. He ain't done too much arena work and he can sometimes drop in on the right shoulder in a turn. I've been workin on it, but he still sometimes forgets about it. When he gets worried he can be a little rushy, but ya only need to feel on one rein to get him to think back to ya. And if ya keep the rhythm ya want him to have he'll find how to get with ya again. He's a good fella who wants to feel right and is always searchin for what feel's best. He never switches off. I think ya'll enjoy him. Why don't we have a session tomorrow and I'll show what I mean?"

"Yeah okay."

The next day I met Walt in the arena and Moz was already saddled and ready to go. Walt rode him first so he could show me what he had been working on and what things I should be prioritizing when I rode. As always Walt rode like he was doing nothing and he and the horse looked like they were part of each other. I wondered whether I will ever be able to ride like that.

When Walt rode up to the fence he stepped off the horse and onto the fence
rail and sat there.

"Your turn, matey."

I will never forget my first ride on Moz. I've had a lot of excellent rides on wonderful horses in my life and most of them are bunched together in my memory like the colours in a beautiful posy of flowers. But the very first time I rode Moz stands out from all of them. I suddenly understood the feeling of having a horse "right there under me". He was ever attentive and ever ready. When I asked him to do something it was never an interruption to what he was doing because he was constantly feeling back to me for what I might ask him to do next. I felt totally inadequate and incompetent because I could feel Moz's confusion when I wasn't as clear as Walt had been. But I also felt the enormous amount of filling in that Moz was doing to make up for my amateur attempts. This little paint had a very sensitive mind, but he did his best to keep a lid on the worry that I was causing. Riding Moz was the coolest thing I had ever felt in my short life. When I got off I was still on a cloud of excitement.

Walt told me to just keep riding him and spend the next week or two getting familiar with each other before adventuring off into new territories of training. He kept saying what a big favour I was doing him, but I kept thinking what a favour Walt was doing for me. It was months before I learned that today was the first day of a master plan that Walt and Amos had concocted.

As I promised Walt, I rode Moz at least three times a week and sometimes more. We were really getting to know each other and after about a month I almost began to think of him as my horse. With Walt's grandfatherly advice from time to time Moz's work was progressing well. After about three months of regular riding there were still no potential buyers for Moz. In fact not one person had come out to look at him. Walt said he didn't understand it, but seem to think there was just a down turn in the market right now.

I had been riding a few horses for other people in the last couple of years and even taking some to shows to compete. I had had reasonable success and I thought I would really like to take Moz to a show or two. I had been doing some jumping at home with him and he was taking to it really well. Being a sensitive horse he was really careful over the jumps, but he wasn't hanging back and he had a classical bascule in the air that really stretched. I thought he might have some potential - at least as a C grader. Walt and Amos agreed to let me compete at the upcoming French's Forest gymkhana.

The gymkhana grounds were close enough to the riding school that I could ride there in about 45 minutes which was just as well because Walt and Amos were too busy to go. We entered in three events and won one and came second in the other two. This qualified us for the championship event, which we won. I rode Moz home with all four ribbons tied around his neck so that anybody driving or walking past could see I was riding a championship horse. I was so excited that mum was going to have sew all my buttons back on my short.

When I got back to the riding school I made sure I rode slowly around the stables and arena so that everybody could see us. People congratulated me and patted Moz as if we had won an Olympic medal. I saw Walt and Amos cleaning their paddock. They looked up at the grin on my face and then I saw a grin come on their faces. Walt tipped his old stained hat at me and went back to cleaning. It was all he needed to say.

Later in the week I spoke to Walt about doing more jumping with Moz and maybe taking him to more shows. I was still elated after the weekend.

"That'll be alright matey, I suppose. But remember he's sensitive and ya need to pace the amount and size his jumpin."

For a while I was keeping the jumps pretty small and working on his technique over bounce fences and grids. Moz was lapping it up and showing real talent. Our next show he won two events, including a six bar and came home with reserve champion. In the shows that followed we always came away with a haul of ribbons and never without at least one blue. Moz was particularly showing a talent for six bar events, which was all right with me because I didn't have to stress about remembering the course.

At home I was jumping him about twice a week and making the practice fences more technical as well as going up in height and width. After all, Moz was progressing so fast that we were being pushed into a higher grade and we were going to have to work harder if we were to remain competitive. I have to say I really loved the challenge and Moz was doing everything I asked of him. Plus everybody knew Moz because of his colour and people were always asking me how he was going. We were becoming local celebrities.

TRAINING MOZ

As the jumps were becoming bigger I had to push Moz a little harder towards them. He needed more forward in order to make it clear over some of the combination fences. It didn't seem to bother him too much and the extra impulsion really helped him make the striding between the fences easier. But I did notice he also made him a little less responsive to the reins when I needed to check him back at times. At first it was not a problem to use a little more hand with him. However, there was a subtle change developing that started me thinking about using a different bit to give me a bit more handle in front of the jumps. I didn't tell Walt about the problem or about changing bits. Walt was busy with other horses and hardly ever saw me working with Moz, so I figured he didn't need to be bothered with a problem I knew I could handle myself.

The show season was coming to an end and I wanted to finish with as many points as I could and maybe have a chance of an award at the showjumping club dinner. The final competition for the year was a big one and I had entered in four events. In the first event we came fourth and the second event we came second place with one rail down. The third event I don't really remember very much. Moz and I were approaching a triple bar and I think I felt him shift to the right in front of the jump.

I woke up in a public ward at the Royal North Shore Hospital. The curtains were drawn around the bed and mum and dad and my sister were standing around. When they saw my eyes open mum grabbed my hand and told dad to get a doctor. Mum asked me questions about how I felt and gave me reassuring kisses that everything would be okay. The doctor came and checked me over then I fell asleep. I woke up again a few hours later. Mum was still beside my bed holding my hand. I asked her what happened.

"You fell off the horse and went through a jump. But we'll talk about it later. You're okay. You just need to rest."

"Is Moz okay?" I asked

"He's fine baby. Your both fine. Walt is outside. Do you want to see him?" mum asked.

"What's he doing here?" I asked I was afraid to see him. I had screwed up with Moz. I had ruined Walt's horse – the best horse I had ever ridden. I had done something terrible and I knew he would hate me. I couldn't bear it if Walt hated me.

"Walt's been here since they brought you into the hospital. He's been waiting for hours and wouldn't go home. Amos is with him too. I think you should let him say hi," mum said.

"Okay."

I was afraid.

Mum left through the curtain and a few minutes later I saw Walt's wrinkled hand split the curtain apart a little. As he started to appear I felt tears begin to well up in my eyes. I don't know where they came from, but I couldn't stop them. My bottom lip was quivering and my nose began to run. The tears were now forming rivulets down my cheeks. Walt looked at me. He looked worried. I was trying my best not to cry, but it was unstoppable. As I opened my mouth to speak my eyes streamed with tears uncontrollably.

"I'm sorry Walt. I'm so sorry. I'm so sorry."

"Don't cry matey. What are ya sorry for? Don't cry," Walt pleaded with a worried expression.

"Walt, I ruined your horse. Moz is the best horse I have ever ridden and I pushed him too hard, too fast. I made him stop at the jump. I did it. I wrecked him. I'm so sorry," I sobbed through the tears.

"Ya don't need to worry about that. Moz will be alright. You'll be jumpin him again. Ya made a mistake in front of a jump. Everybody does that some time. Ya just hurtin. You'll be alright and so will Moz. You quit ya tears or them nurses will put ya in the baby ward."

Mum said that I should get my rest and that Walt and Amos could visit tomorrow. I don't remember too much of the stay in hospital. I guess concussion is like that. I stayed for about 3 days and I know Walt and Amos came to visit at least one other time, but I don't remember what we talked about. I remember dad and mum arguing about whether or not I should be allowed to ride again. Dad was adamant that I give up riding, but mum had her ways of weakening dad's determination and I knew the ban from going to the riding school would only last a couple of weeks.

When the ban was eventually lifted, the first one I went to see was Moz. He looked fine and even came to the gate for a scratch on the poll, his favourite spot. I then went to see the boss and he said not to worry about coming back to work in a hurry. My job was safe and he would manage for another week or two if I just wanted to hang out with the horses. I told him I felt fine and that I only showed up because I missed cleaning the stables so much. I got the barrow and fork and headed for the far stables to make a start on Milly's stall.

I had already shifted one barrow load when I turned to see Walt standing in the doorway.

"Weren't ya gonna to come and see me and Amos to say hello?"

"Sorry Walt. I was going to do that, but the boss wanted me to start straight away on the stables. I was going to come and see you. Honest!" I replied.

"Well matey, a fellow could get a complex that maybe ya was avoidin him. Amos and me called ya at home a few times, but ya ain't never called back. I figured ya was mad at me."

"What? No Walt. I'm not mad. That's crazy. Why would you think that?"

"Well matey, what's wrong? Somethin is wrong. I know ya well enough to know that."

"Nothing. Nothing's wrong," I lied.

"C'mon. Tell me. What's wrong?"

"Well, it's not you at all. I'm not mad at you. I'm mad at myself. I feel ashamed. I feel terrible," I said meekly.

"But why matey? Ya only had a fall. Everybody has a fall. It ain't nothin to be ashamed about. I'm sorry ya got hurt, but it ain't a big deal," Walt exclaimed.

"Crashing through the fence is not what I am ashamed about, Walt. The reason I feel so bad is because of why Moz ran out on the fence."

I began to feel the tears coming back. I tried to hold them in, but I felt I was losing the battle.

"I knew Moz was getting more worried about jumping. The jumps were getting bigger and courses were getting harder. Moz was trying his heart out, but he wasn't ready. He began to rush in front of jumps and wouldn't listen to the reins and then between jumps he was holding back and wouldn't listen to my legs. I never told you, but I had to change bits to get more control of Moz in front of the jumps. I knew these problems were developing, but we were getting to the end of the show season and another couple of wins would put us ahead in the club championships."

"Matey, I knew ya had changed bits and I knew ya was havin problems. Ya don't always see me, but I'm always watchin. I was waitin for ya to come and talk to me about it. But ya didn't. Why not?"

"I don't know Walt. I guess I figured I could work on fixing the problems after the show season ended. I just needed a few more points to finish up the season and I thought once that is done and we have the championship I would have plenty of time to work with Moz before the next season. I was going to get you to help me fix all the undoing I had done."

"Winning is that important to ya, is it?" Walt asked.

"Well, competing is so much fun. I really love it and when we come home with ribbons it feels fantastic," I answered.

"Does it feel just as good when ya don't go home with any ribbons?" was Walt's next question.

"Well, no. I guess losing is not nearly as much fun as winning Walt."

"So ya sayin the amount of pleasure ya get from ridin Moz depends on whether he wins a competition or not. Is that it, matey?"

"Well, no. It's not like that. Well maybe. But it's not as simple as that." I tried to clutch for the right answer.

"Matey, d'ya remember the first time ya rode Moz?"

"Yeah. I remember."

"D'ya remember how much fun ya said it was? How it was the best ride ya had ever had. D'ya remember?"

"Yes. I remember that!" I said slightly irritated.

"Is it still the best ride ya have ever had, matey?"

"I dunno. I guess so," I said.

"There weren't no blue ribbons at the end of that ride if I recall rightly," Walt stated. "That was a fun ride 'cause ya felt somethin that a horse could give ya that ya ain't ever felt before. Ya felt Moz give over more of himself than ya had ever felt any horse give before. It was special."

"Yeah. I guess so Walt"

"Matey, have ya felt Moz give that much or more in the last few months?"

TRAINING MOZ

"No Walt. I guess not. I guess if anything he has given less. The only thing Moz has given me more of is resistance and worry. I know that. I know I screwed up. That's why I feel ashamed. He is your horse and you trusted me with him and I let you down. It's not me being mad at you. It's you that should be mad at me. I'm sorry."

"Matey, the only thing ya should feel ashamed about is being a teenager. But that ain't ya fault. When it comes to competition, lots of people let their ego get in the way of their horsemanship. Ribbons validate our skill as horse people to the rest of the world. It's a measure of talent that we can show people. But it's fake. Horses don't care about ribbons or comin first or last.

"There ain't nothin wrong with competin or in winnin ribbons. It's all okay. But when the competition gets to bein more important than the horse, then ya have lost ya way in my book. Nothin is more important than ya horse and ya horsemanship. There will always be other shows and other chances to win ribbons. But if ya horse ain't right, if he's tellin ya somethin is wrong and ya ain't listenin then ya ain't ever gonna feel what ya felt on that first ride. And you already know that was the best feelin ya ever had in the saddle. Why would ya ever want to sacrifice that for a piece of ribbon ya could buy in a shop for a dollar?"

"I know Walt. I know you're right. I'm sorry. I'm so sorry. I don't blame you if you never let me near Moz again. I wish I could do it all over again, but I can't and I'm sorry."

"I know ya are, matey. I know. But listen. I still need ya to work him til I find a buyer. Me and Amos will help ya get Moz on track again, but would ya do that for me?"

"Are you sure, Walt?"

"Yeah, I reckon it's a good idea."

"Okay. That'd be great. But are you ever going to be able to sell him? It's been about a year now and nobody has even come to look at him."

"Well matey, to be honest we ain't be lookin too hard for a buyer. Me and Amos reckoned you could do with a good honest horse like Moz to teach somethin about committin to a horse over the long term. I think it's a lesson ya startin to learn so we will be lookin for a buyer soon. But until then ya need to put some time into him."

I was very excited, but scared about working Moz again. It seemed an even bigger responsibility now than it did when Walt first asked me a year ago. I desperately didn't want to screw up again. Walt helped me work on getting Moz to let go of his anxiety and soften his thoughts. He was such a terrific horse that it took less time than I imagined possible. I did get to jump him again in a couple of shows and we did pretty well. But Walt and Amos needed to sell him and so I had to let him go. Fortunately, the boss bought him for his daughter and I was able to see him all the time and he had a good life.

I look back now at what the old brothers did and feel ashamed that at the time I never appreciated my good fortune at having Walt and Amos in my life. The way they guided and guarded me was enough to make a fellow think they cared.

CHASING A REACTION

It was suppose to be a secret. I had never told anybody. The horses and Walt and Amos were not the only reasons I wanted to hang around the riding school. There was a girl. I really liked her, but it was a secret. Nobody knew. I was fifteen and she was a couple of months younger than me. Somehow I found reasons to chip weeds near the arena when she was riding her horse. Nobody could have guessed that it wasn't just coincidence that I happened to clean saddles right by the spot she liked to sit to eat her sandwich. And I was so casual about bumping into her and saying "hi" twenty times a day that anybody watching would never have thought I had a crush on her.

My relationship with Natalie was intense. I knew we were destined to be happy together forever – if only she could remember my name! No – it wasn't that bad. I did really like her, but it seemed that her take on me was that I was like the fellow that was friends with her old brother. We talked and got along okay, but no more than I did with any of the other regular girls that hung around the riding school. Then one day my chance to get closer to Nat came along.

Walt and Amos were taking me to a local show. I was jumping a big thoroughbred named Henry. We had had good success around the local jumping circuit and Henry was steadily climbing through the grades. Actually, he was too successful and his rapid rise into the higher grades was causing us some problems. But that is a story for another time.

I knew Nat was also going to the same show to compete in a couple of Galloway classes with her horse, Cinnamon. (a.k.a. Cindy). I hoped we might be able to spend some time hanging out together at the show without all the other girls from the riding school being around. About a week before the show Natalie told me she couldn't go because her brother was in the soccer grand final on the same day and her family wanted to watch him play. This meant she had nobody to take her to the show. I felt more than a little disappointed. I'm sure the Oxford Dictionary defines hope "as a teenage boy with a crush."

I walked away pretty despondent until I suddenly had a major brainstorm.

"Hey Nat, why don't you come to the show with us in the truck? There's plenty of room for Cindy."

"I don't know. I don't know if my parents will let me. Will it be okay with Walt and Amos?" Natalie asked.

"They won't mind. You talk to your parents tonight and I'll talk to Walt and Amos. If you promise to buy Amos a pie for lunch he'll drive you to every show in the country," I told her.

It was settled. Nat's folks rang Walt and Amos and cleared it with them. I had already sounded out the old brothers about my stroke of genius and knew they were okay with it. But I was so casual about the way I presented the idea to them, they had no clue it was part of my brilliant scheme to get closer to the prettiest girl in the world.

All week I was excited about the weekend. I would daydream about how much fun Nat and I would have at the show. I wanted it to be the best day ever and made sure all my competition gear looked new and my boots shined like a mirror. Henry's saddle and bridle were cleaned and oiled and I even bought a new saddlecloth for the occasion. It was a very busy week and I really didn't have as much time to work with Henry as I would normally. But I knew he was going well and besides I really didn't want to win any events for a while to avoid us being promoted up a grade again.

I didn't sleep much the night before the show. But I was still up early and ready. Natalie was waiting when I got to the riding school – she looked a dream. Cindy was already plaited and groomed. I quickly got all the gear into the truck and Henry ready. By the time the old men arrived we only had to load the horses and we were off. Walt drove and I sat between Amos and Natalie. It was a squeeze and I couldn't have been happier.

As soon as we found a parking spot under a big elm tree we unloaded the horses. Cindy came off feeling mellow, but Henry charged down the ramp like a boxer who had just heard the bell. He was full of fight. He wasn't normally like this, but he had campaigned enough that I knew he would settle soon.

I didn't have too long before my first event, so I figured I should get Henry saddled and warmed up immediately. He wouldn't stand still while I brushed him and he nearly knocked me sideways with his rear end when I lifted the saddle onto his back. He was more distracted and lost than I had ever seen. I knew I just had to get him saddled then work him to get his mind back on the game before our event, otherwise he'd be crashing through fences and running off course.

I took him over to the warm-up ring and he was even worse. He jumped around like a hopping mouse being chased by a fox. Whenever another horse came close he shied. I think somebody must have complained about us because a steward came over and asked us to leave the warm-up ring as we were upsetting the other horses. I was looking around for Walt or Amos because I was beginning to feel that I was losing Henry more and more. I don't know what his problem was, but he was ruining the good impression I was hoping to make with Natalie.

There was a small area behind the parking barrier where nobody was riding, so I took Henry over there hoping that Walt and Amos were coming too, but equally hoping that Nat was too busy to be watching us. Henry was prancing all the way and I kept turning him to try to get him to walk. Then he would suddenly shy at something invisible to humans. When I tried to turn him from running sideways he would kick out or pig root. When I tried to back him up he nearly reared. When I tried to do a hindquarter disengagement he almost fell over. A one rein stop made him even more upset. Henry was not listening to me at all. He felt he needed to be in full flight mode and I was interfering with that. Although I was still alive I was not certain how long this would last. It seemed that everything I did just made Henry more upset. Where were the brothers?

I knew I had to get control of Henry and settled because my event was starting and I hadn't even done one warm up fence - and I was the third competitor! I really felt it was time to give up and forget about jumping today. Then I heard Walt's voice.

"Why ya hidin over here, matey? They've called ya three times."

"I can't get him to settle, Walt. I don't know what to do. I can't jump him like this. What do I do?"

"Come here, matey. Stay sittin in the saddle and I'll just take them reins, you let 'em go and just hang on to ya saddle," Walt said.

I rode up to Walt. Henry was a bit wary and needed some urging to go straight up to the old man. Walt reached out and stroked Henry's forehead. Walt and Henry were facing each other head to head as Walt put his left hand round the left rein near the buckle that attached to the ring of the bit. I felt Henry brace up immediately. He tightened dramatically through his back. Henry pulled against Walt's hand and Walt held firm. When Henry tried to shift back a step, Walt firmly insisted he lean his weight forward. He didn't ask for a step, just for Henry to lean forward. When Henry tried to move his feet, Walt again held the rein with no give and Henry rocked his weight back again. Walt then used the rein to ask Henry to shift his weight onto his front end, but Henry rocked even further back. Walt matched the resistance until Henry leaned forward, then he softened his hand. Henry tried once more to step forward. He just knew he had to move and rocking his weight back and forth was not satisfying Henry's need to move his feet. But Walt held firm again like he was an immovable rock and Henry leaned back. The next time Walt asked Henry to shift his weight onto his forehand, it weighed nothing in Walt's hand. At the very same time I felt Henry almost completely let down. Walt then asked Henry to move one leg forward and stop. It moved with all the resistance of a party balloon swaying in a soft breeze. There was no argument. Walt then asked Henry to take one step back and it happened as if it was Henry's idea. Next Walt was getting Henry to move his hind end across one step; and his forehand; and then a complete side pass in either direction. It didn't trouble Henry one bit.

"Okay matey, I think ya alright now."

"Wow, Walt. What did you do?" I asked.

"Not much. It's an old trick I learned from the Eskimos. Ya didn't know them Eskimos are great horse trainers, did ya?"

The smirk on his face told me just to leave it for now and pick his brain later.

I had missed my first event, but didn't have long to wait until the next event. Henry was a different horse. He cleared everything the first round and in the second round I had to make sure I took the long course to avoid going too fast. We came fourth and I was really happy.

Natalie had already had one event by the time I had competed. She got called in by the judge, but placed fifth. We didn't get to have lunch together or hang out because our event times kept clashing. This gave me time to think more about Henry and try to find out from Walt what I had been missing.

"Walt, why was Henry so crazy this morning? He is never like that and even when he is having a bad day I can always get him settled pretty quickly."

"Matey, I don't know why he was bothered this morning. But it don't matter why. Knowin the reason doesn't help fix the problem. A fellows got to deal with what is in front of him at the time. It don't help wonderin what set it off."

"Well, then what did you do that I didn't that made the difference to him?" I asked. "Was it just that you were really quiet about what you did and I was doing too much?"

"Nah, I don't think it was so much that. You were doin a lot. There was quite a dust storm around you two. But I reckon you was always behind what was happenin. Henry would shy and ya'd shut it down. Henry would get scared of a horse and ya'd try shut it down. Henry would dance around like a ballerina with a bladder problem and ya'd try to shut it down. Ya was always reactin to what he was doin. That thoroughbred would do somethin and ya'd jump in tryin to control it."

"What should I have done Walt?"

"What Henry needed was somebody to tell him he didn't need to feel that way. You let him feel that way and then reacted to what them feelins made him do. When I took a hold of them reins and Henry said he needed to push forward, I said 'no, ya don't need to feel that way – stop pushin.' Then he would say he needed to go back and I'd hold them reins and say 'no, ya don't need to feel that way – stop pullin and let go of them feelins.' Henry would keep shiftin around and I kept blockin him, tellin him that right there in my hand is where he needs to be. I kept usin them reins to tell him 'no need to feel that bad, stop feelin that way and be soft here with me.

"Pretty soon Henry began to melt in my hand. He'd let go of them feelins that made him feel he needed to jump around and shy at shadows. He turned his busy mind into a quiet mind. Then when I said to him he could move, I was able to direct them feet back or forward, left or right. He had shaken off all the trouble inside of him that got in the way of him listenin to me. He didn't feel he needed to run for his life from every little thing that caught his attention. Now he was available to be directed to anywhere I liked. There was no fight."

"But how is that different to what I was trying to do, Walt?"

"Well matey, as I said ya was reactin to his reaction. Henry would jump and then ya tried to do somethin about it. Then he did somethin else and ya reacted to that. Change for Henry was only goin to come either with a whole lot of time or with all the jumpin around causin him to get too tired to jump around anymore.

"But what I was doin was tryin not let him go to that bad place that made him spit the dummy. Instead of waitin for him to do somethin, I was usin them reins to give him somethin to think about and tellin him that the reaction he wanted to have wasn't goin to work out so he had better change them feelins. Most of us spend our lives catchin up to a horse's reaction and too few of us take the time to change the feelins that cause the reaction before the reaction turns into action. It's what ya do before he has the reaction that makes the difference."

It gave me a lot to think about. In fact, I was thinking about it and analysing what had happened when I saw Nat coming towards me with a big blue ribbon around Cindy's neck. So much had happened that day that I had forgotten to go along and cheer Nat along in her last event. Nat had a skip in her step and a huge grin on her already perfect face.

"Look at what we won! I've never come first before. I'm so excited."

Nat threw her arms around me and gave me a huge hug which didn't seem to last long enough - until she followed it with a kiss on the cheek. I was mortified with embarrassment.

Amos gave me a sly wink and said, "I reckon the transport fella should get one of them too."

Nat gave both Amos and Walt a hug. But I was the only one that got a kiss.

It was a great day. I learned something incredibly important about helping a troubled horse and I got a kiss from Nat. It couldn't have turned out better. And I was sure nobody knew I had a crush on the girl.

CHARLIE

Nowadays there are houses and schools all over where the riding school used to be. The local school use to be a 1 room, 1 teacher centre of learning, but now it is a multi-storey, multi-building college of advanced education. Where wallabies and wombats used to roam in the hills there are manicured lawns with closely fenced yards to keep the pet poodle in and the neighbours out. The riding trails have been turned into dark grey motor ways and instead of fallen trees and ditches to negotiate there are traffic lights and roundabouts.

The riding school is not the only forgotten treasure to have succumbed to our ravenous hunger for urban expansion. Surrounding the riding school were hundreds of acres of orchards that each year provided Sydney with an abundant supply of apples, citrus and stone fruit. As a kid it was ritual to pilfer ripe fruit from the ground and occasionally from the trees. Old Mr Barnsby never seemed to mind even when he caught you doing it. It was pretty much accepted that that was the sort of relationship the Barnsby's had with the kids and locals in the area.

The boss of the riding school had a cousin called Charlie. Charlie was an itinerant. He travelled all over the country going from job to job and living day to day. Charlie drove an old Bedford truck with a rough sort of living quarters in the back of the truck. He also travelled with his best companion, a mule called Suzy, which came along in the float that it towed behind the Bedford.

Charlie was an interesting fellow and as a kid he sort of scared me. He was in his late forties or early fifties, tall and heavy. He always had a 3-day-old beard and wore torn and stained T-shirts and ripped jeans. He looked unclean and there was a constant whiff of body odour about him. When he talked to you there was always a hint of white spit at the corner of his mouth. Charlie used to be a policeman and at one time had a wife and 2 kids. While on duty Charlie got called out to a brawl in a pub in Newtown and during the skirmish a bottle was smashed over his head and he hit the ground headfirst. He was in hospital for 4 months and rehab for another 12 months. The damage to his brain was permanent and he would never be able to work again. About 18 months after he was allowed home, his wife took the kids and left. He never saw his kids again. Charlie was left to fend for himself on a pension. After a couple of years being cooped up in a flat in Bondi, Charlie bought the truck and went looking for jobs picking fruit in the country.

At one farm in the Riverina he saw and fell in love with Suzy. She was a 15hh mule that had no purpose in life anymore. Charlie had to have her and the farmer said he could take her if he could ride her. Charlie had never ridden in his life and didn't know a thing about it. Without even asking the owner to borrow a saddle or bridle, Charlie got some hay twine and led Suzy over to a rail fence. He clumsily climbed the fence and leapt across her back. Suzy just stood quietly and waited until Charlie was sitting up and balanced. She walked him around as Charlie clung to her neck. When she stopped by the stump, Charlie slid off and fell to the ground laughing. He was in love. Apparently the farmer was dumbfounded because Suzy had not been ridden for five years and even then had been a handful. He let Charlie take her.

Every year Charlie showed up at the riding school ready for apple picking season. The boss let him park his truck near the house so he could connect to power and use the toilet and shower. He gave Suzy her own yard too. Each morning Charlie would go off to pick apples, but on Sundays he would hang around the riding school. That's how I got to know him.

I use to watch Charlie with Suzy. I was constantly amazed how patient that animal was with him. I had never seen somebody so clueless of how to be around a horse or a mule. It was the funniest ritual to see them together. He was so clumsy at mounting. He would haul his huge mass up like he was doing chin-ups. He always accidentally kicked Suzy in the ribs as he got on board. You could see her flinch, but she never budged. She would wait until she was sure he was on and safe. Once she was sure everything was okay, she would walk off without waiting for him to give the all clear. She would head straight for the sweetest grass, put her head down and begin to eat. Charlie would pull the reins to get her head up, kick her and say "Aw Suzy, don't eat. Come on Suzy. SUZY!" Then Suzy would pick her head up and walk on. It was like that virtually every time I saw them.

Charlie had almost no balance and would sway constantly in the saddle. If he wanted to change direction or stop he just jerked on the reins and say "Aw come on Suzy." If Suzy ever trotted Charlie would let go of the reins and lean forward to wrap his arms around her neck and say "Aw Suzy slow down," and wait until she slowed to a walk again. I can't imagine what he would have done if Suzy had ever got a wild idea to canter.

One day Charlie approached Walt about how to teach Suzy to kneel down. He had seen a fellow get a horse to kneel down and then get on and figured that if he could teach that to Suzy he would not have to always be looking for something to climb onto before getting on Suzy.

"Charlie, no worries. I can teach Suzy to kneel for ya. But it will cost ya some of them apples ya been pickin," Walt said.

"No Walt. Suzy don't like too many other people. She's a woman ya know and she's very fussy. Just tell me what I'm suppose to do and I'll teach her," Charlie laughed. Charlie was always laughing.

Walt explained about teaching her to softly pick up a front leg and get her to put weight on that shoulder as the leg is off the ground. He emphasized about helping to prepare her hindquarters to reach back so she would stretch her front end down and forward. Walt gave Charlie some suggestions of techniques to get this done. As Walt talked Charlie just nodded, but didn't ask any questions.

"Okay Walt, I think I got it now. I'll just go and explain it to Suzy," he said.

At first watching Charlie train Suzy to kneel down was a frustrating experience. Suzy was standing in her yard with no halter or lead rope. Charlie picked up her left foreleg in his hand and then reached across her wither and tried to pull her towards him. It was clear that the only thing Charlie had heard of Walt's explanation is to pick up a foot and get the horse to lean on it while it is up.

"Aw Suzy. Come on Suzy. Go down Suzy. Come on, go down. Good girl, go down Suzy."

This went on for several minutes. Charlie just persisted and persisted with the same approach. The frustration of seeing this was driving me nuts. Just when I was about to walk away because I couldn't watch anymore, Suzy kneeled. I didn't even see her get ready. She just did it. What made me even more bug eyed was the instant she kneeled Charlie threw a leg over her and climb on. There was no reward or release of pressure for kneeling down. Charlie figured that kneeling was just part of the job and the other part was getting on. So he just did it. He sat up there laughing, slapping her neck and yelling "Good girl Suzy. Good girl." I told Charlie I thought that was amazing and then I ran off to tell Walt.

"Walt, I can't believe it, you should have seen it. Charlie got Suzy to kneel down. He had no idea what he was doing and hardly took in anything you had told him, but he trained her to kneel. It was amazing," I said in my excitement.

"That's great matey," he said.

"Yeh, it was incredible because he did almost everything wrong, yet she still kneeled for him. I don't understand it. I don't understand Walt. How can a person be so un-horsey, so clumsy and have so little understanding as Charlie and still get along so well with his mule?" I asked.

"Matey, Charlie sure is different. His accident left him a little slower than most and more clumsy than most, but it didn't change anythin that's inside him. There ain't any doubt that there are lots of mules and horses that wouldn't be able to get along nearly so well with Charlie as Suzy does. But ya know matey what he has to offer Suzy is what Suzy most needs. Charlie gives her the care and love she needs and she knows his intent is always good and that she comes first in his list of what is important. For her it's a small price to pay to put up with him nearly fallin

CHARLIE

off every step or jerkin her in the mouth. I don't know why Suzy needs somebody like Charlie, but it works for her and they are lucky to have each other. Lots of us try to make the horse be what we want them to be and not enough of us try to be the person our horses need us to be. There is a lot to be learned from a fellow like Charlie.

THE PLIGHT OF ENRICO

You don't see many Haflinger horses in Australia. Even fewer when I was a kid than nowadays. So when a Haflinger gelding named Enrico arrived at the riding school it caught my attention. Enrico had been bought by Laura who was a very nice lady in her late thirties. She had seen him in a paddock every day for months and finally got the nerve to go to the house near the paddock and ask if he was for sale. Laura had grown up in France (her dad was a diplomat) and she had great childhood memories of riding through the countryside of Normandy on her Haflinger mare.

Enrico's owners were very glad to be rid of him. He had been bought from a dealer for their daughter, but it had all gone terribly wrong from day one. Enrico was almost impossible to catch and when he was finally caught he couldn't stand still long enough to get a saddle on. The owners had had enough and wanted him gone. They said that if Laura could catch him, she could have him. Well, it took some doing, but after finally running him into a neighbour's stockyard and getting a rope around his neck, Enrico was caught. Laura later told me it took three large fellows to manhandle the little 13.2 hh Enrico into a truck. And that's how he came to be at the riding school.

It got to see quite a lot of Enrico because he was kept in a yard about a half the size of a tennis court and it was my job to feed him and clean his yard each day. He was a very skittish little guy and would take off to the far end of the pen and shake whenever I entered. Laura didn't have much luck with him either. Every day she came and tried to approach him, but every day poor Enrico would run wildly as if being chased by the devil with a pitch fork. After a bit Laura would leave in frustration. It wasn't too many days before Laura was telling me that she wondered if she had done the right thing by taking him.

I had almost the opposite approach from Laura. I would enter his yard with a wheelbarrow and manure fork and go about my business. I would let him run to the far end of the yard and figured that eventually he would be so use to the routine that he would soon realise that I was no threat to his safety. Each day Laura did her thing and each day I did my thing. Laura started using food as an enticement to ease Enrico's worry and it made some change in him. But after three weeks it never got a whole lot better. Enrico would sneak a bite of food and jump away before Laura could touch him. And if she did move when he was nearby he would take off running.

I too wasn't making fast progress. Enrico got better to the point that he would see me approaching the yard with the wheelbarrow and before I entered he would wander to the far end of the yard. But at least he wasn't running wildly like he did the first few days. I still couldn't get close to him without him shaking and threatening to jump over the top rail.

I didn't realise that Walt was behind me one day when I was cleaning out Enrico's yard.

"How ya goin with the taffy fellow, Matey?" he asked.

"Ah Walt, he is still really scared and won't let anybody near him. Are all Haflinger's like this?"

"Well Matey, I ain't seen too many of 'em, but ya know they were bred for carryin packs in them Austrian mountains, so I expect they would normally have pretty steady minds," he answered.

"Well, this one hasn't. He must've got swindled when they handed out brains."

"I wouldn't judge him too harshly, matey. I think ya can be pretty sure somebody has taught this little fellow to be as scared as he is," Walt surmised.

"Do you think he can be helped, Walt?"

"Sure, matey."

"How?" I asked.

THE PLIGHT OF ENRICO

"Change how he's feelin," Walt said as if the answer was too obvious and wasn't I stupid for not knowing that.

"Yeah, but how?" I asked.

"Well, don't let him feel that bad."

I was beginning to feel like I was missing the obvious here and Walt was trying to explain to me that water was wet.

"Okay, Walt let's start from the start. I do not understand the point you are making here. How do I get a horse that is scared of people change to be not scared of people," I asked in the hope of an answer that would make sense to me?

"Alright matey, let's take the way you clean the yard as an example."

"Okay," I said.

"Well matey, why does the horse run to the other end of the yard from ya when you come in?" he asked.

"Because it is the furthest point from me and he feel's safer being far away from people," I answered.

"That's right, but why does he still do it after three weeks of the same pattern? Why ain't he learned that ya ain't gonna kill him and he don't need to run to the other side?"

"I don't know. Because he's dumb?"

"No matey. It's because it works for him. When he first arrived and ya came into the yard, he ran to the other end. Ya left the yard and he was still alive. Ya taught him that if he goes to the other side of the yard when ya come in he will survive. So each day when ya take that wheel barra into the yard he wanders over to where he knows he will be safe. It is a pattern that has successively repeated itself over and over for three weeks. He has learned what he needs to do to stay safe, so why should he change it? If he changes the pattern, he knows there is a possibility he might die. So he figures when ya on a good thing, stick to it."

"I never thought of it like that, Walt."

"That's because ya think like a human does instead of how a horse does, matey."

"What can I do to help him?" I asked.

"Well, the horse runs to the other side of the pen because he thinks that works for him. Change that. Show him it don't work for him."

"How do I do that, Walt?"

"Lots of ways, matey. For instance, when he runs to the other side, go towards the other side and make like ya have to pick up poo nearby. When he runs somewhere else, head that way as if ya have to go and check if that fence rail has a nail stickin out. When he goes somewhere else, wander over there and see if ya dropped ya watch on the ground not far from there. Let him work out that runnin ain't workin. But don't do so much that ya force him to jump out of the yard or run ya down. Do enough to get him to search for another strategy other than runnin to the opposite end, but not so much that he thinks he will die. Eventually, he will figure out takin off to the far side ain't workin and he will take a moment when he will stand facin ya and look at ya. That's when ya walk away. Build on that each day until in a couple of weeks ya will walk into the yard and he will stand quietly and check ya out. Then ya on the way to him feelin it's ok to be caught."

Of course I needed to get Laura to go along with this new strategy because we both had to be consistent if it was to work. She was very excited because she could see the sense in Walt's thinking. It took about a week and a half before both Laura and I could walk into the yard and approach Enrico to pat him.

It has been a long personal journey to understand the concept that I could effect a change in a horse's feelings by teaching him that the feelings he has don't work or are not in his best interest. He can change the way he feels and change his ideas because I can show him a different way to respond which will work better for him. I'm not talking about just teaching him to do what I want him to do, but to actually change his feelings about what I want him to do. This is a tough concept to grasp. I wish I understood it better than I do. But I think each year and each horse gives me more insight.

PICKINESS

A few months ago I was giving a lesson to a student that had been working with me for more than a year. We were starting to look at changes of lead and her horse was having a few problems getting her body shaped up for the transition. It struck me that the problem was actually coming from a resistance the mare was having to yielding her hindquarters during the change of flexion. My student, Libby was getting pretty frustrated with the whole thing and I suggested we go back a few steps and look at Penny's hindquarter work again. It was obvious that Libby was not impressed with my suggestion, but she humoured me and gave it a try. As soon as she did it was like a lightning strike as to what was the problem. Penny's hindquarters were not yielding freely and she resisted Libby's attempt to shift them from right to left and back to the right again. It wasn't terrible, but there was certainly some resistance.

The rest of the session was taken up with freeing Penny's hindquarters, followed by change of flexions at the trot. At the end of the lesson Libby asked the inevitable question about why we were working on yielding up the hindquarters when that was something that we worked on months and months ago. I'm not sure my answer gave her much comfort or satisfaction, but it relates to something I tell students and clients over and over again. It was something that Walt told to me when I asked a similar question.

I was then a kid in my late teens and for some time people had been paying me to ride, train and compete on their horses. I loved the extra money, but most of all I loved the work. It was better than just breaking in a horse for somebody because those horses were always going home just when they were starting to work well and becoming fun to ride. But with the training and competition horses I got to stay with them for quite awhile. It was fun to ride a horse as it progressed beyond just the very basics.

One horse I had at the time was called Bill and owned by a very nice lady who didn't have time to ride, but liked to see her horse compete. Bill and I had been steadily going up through the ranks of the show jumping rings over many months. His performances were getting better and better with each outing. However, one of his consistent problems was an inability to turn quickly and cut corners when we were against the clock. He was one of those big gangly types that naturally had a wide turning circle. I knew I had to improve on this if we were to advance much further in competition.

I worked pretty hard at teaching Bill to be more responsive at following the feel of the rein and not run through his outside shoulder in the turns even at speed. It became a project that continued for a few weeks without a whole lot of improvement. After feeling that I was not getting the changes I need I finally approached Walt with the problem.

"Well matey, ya kinda got Bill runin through the shoulder 'cause his rear is pushin the shoulder forward and out. The problem ain't so much his shoulder, but his rear. Them reins don't have much meanin to them hindquarters, so when ya ask him to come 'round the corner the rear end is still goin straight."

"So Walt, how do I fix that?"

"Well matey, a lot of folks would tell ya to use more of that outside rein, but that only hides the problem with them hindquarters – it don't fix it. What I would do is get the connection between the rear end and that inside rein by stop doin hindquarter disengagements and start workin on stepping those hind feet over with feel in them reins."

"But Walt, I've done plenty of that sort of stuff. Bill's been doing hindquarters yields, forehand yields, backing in circles, shoulder in, haunches in, over bent circles, counter bent circles etc etc. Everything you and Amos have taught me about the reins and the feet. I don't know what more I can do?"

PICKINESS

"Matey, don't make the mistake of thinkin ya have ever fixed anythin. I ain't ever fixed. Everythin ya teach a horse is only half taught. It ain't ever taught to perfection. Nothin is ever just right and don't ever need to be better. It ain't ever finished."

"That's pretty depressing Walt. You mean that I'll never get it right."

"Well matey, ya will never get it perfect, but ya just might get it good enough to get by with the job ya have in mind. But when ya come across a hiccup, ya might find it pays to go back to the old stuff and try to get it better.

"Ya see matey, the value of any exercise is not in the exercise. The value is in the quality that you do the exercise. It don't matter how many times ya get ya horse to do something, it only has value if he does it right and each time ya ask him he does more right. When ya start out ya horse might be sorta rough whenever ya ask him to do an exercise, but for it to be of any value he's gotta be tryin to get it right. The more ya ask him the better it ought to be gettin. Not much point in askin him to do any exercise if ain't gettin better and better. Ya could do the same exercise every day of ya life and ya ain't ever gonna be perfect, but ya had better be getting better at it or ya probably wastin ya time.

"When ya been workin on all them things with ol' Bill ya probably got them good enough to get ya by with jobs ya been askin him to do. But now that ya is askin him to do better and use his rear quarters in a way that he has never had to before ya find that maybe them hindquarter yields and shoulder in and all the other stuff weren't done with enough quality to get the job done that ya is askin of Bill now. It weren't bad quality before, but now that you need him to make a greater effort, ya need the basic stuff to be even better."

"So what should I do, Walt?

"Well matey, go back to some of them basics and get picky. Bill is far enough along that ya can ask him to do things with more precision and more accuracy. Ask him for more life in them feet, more bend and more softness. Do the same stuff ya did weeks and months back, but ask it to be better. Don't accept just the same old response from him, get picky and ask for a better response. Teach him that the way he was doin it ain't no longer gettin him by and he needs to be reachin a new standard. Don't hassle him and don't pick on him for stuff that is too hard for him, but help him be better so that he is better able to handle the harder work he's goin to have to do down the road. Get picky, but stay fair."

When Libby asked me why I had her doing hindquarter yields during our recent lesson I told her that now that we were asking Penny for lead changes were needed to have more influence in the way she used her hindquarters. I said that we may have been doing the same exercises we did months ago, but we were doing them with a higher quality than we ever did in the past. It was time we got pickier; ask for more precision and accuracy so that Penny could better cope with her new workload. We were doing old stuff better in order to teach her new stuff. I saw Libby's face sag when I added that in a few more months we would probably be re-visiting the same exercises again to get even pickier, when it was time to work on pirouettes. BREAKING IN BOSCO

I hadn't broken in very many horses before I met Bosco. Up to that point most of my experience with starting horses under saddle had been with fairly tame animals and with the help of the old brothers they had been pretty straigh forward. But Bosco was a different story.

He was a 3 year old thoroughbred gelding - not very tall and slight of build. He looked more like a preying mantis than an athlete built for work. But I figured he still had a lot of growing to do and would eventually develop into a lean, mean riding machine. The main problem with Bosco was that he was a bundle of nerves. Anything (and I mean anything) would cause him to leap sideways in the air. In fact, the first two or three sessions I worked with him I reckon he spent more time in the air than on the ground. He was certainly one messed up horse. Walt and Amos helped a lot with teaching me to settle him. They explained to me when to go easy and when to get firm. At first I thought that a horse as nervous and frightened as Bosco required a quiet, gently approach and I tried not to upset him much. But Walt showed me that I was setting him up to stay scared of everything new. Walt explained that I shouldn't creep around him, but be casual and don't take his leaping around as the right answer.

"Matey, ya don't set out to scare him, but ya don't want to be tip toein around him neither. Let him know that this is how life is going to be

PICKINESS

and he can get use to it. Set up for a change and make sure ya get a change in the way he's feelin."

Within a couple of weeks Bosco was settling pretty nicely. He was getting easier to catch. I could ask him to move around the pen without him bolting for his life. He could change direction with some very sweet turns. It was looking pretty good. It now came time for the saddling.

To say that he did not take well to wearing a saddle is an understatement. Once the girth was snugged he shot forward faster and leapt higher than any horse I can remember. He roared, bucked and twisted. For such a little fellow he sure knew how to propel himself. It took many minutes before he stopped running and bucking, but eventually he gathered himself together and I could do some ground exercises with him.

The next day was similar. Again he bucked, roared and twisted with the saddle. It looked just like the first day. I spoke to Walt and Amos after I had hosed Bosco off and put him back in the paddock. They suggested I put a little more pressure on him and give him a reason to not buck. They showed me how to rope the saddle horn, rear cinch and stirrups, as well as to rope his hindquarters. This seemed all cowboy stuff to me and I really didn't understand why I would use a rope.

"Matey, when he goes to buck, pull on the saddle horn with ya rope. Pull hard. When he slows down and stops buckin, ease off the pull on the horn. Repeat it until he stops buckin the second he feels the pressure on the horn. The pull on the saddle will have meanin to him and he will learn to control his buckin. When that looks good do the same by puttin the lariat rope on the stirrup. Pull till he stops buckin. Then when that's workin good, do the same for the rear cinch. When ya got that workin, make a loop in the rope and lay it over his hindquarters just behind the saddle. Let him carry the rope up over his backside and down his legs. Get him used to these strange things that bother him so much. He needs to change the way he feels about being saddled and carrying that hunk of leather. If ya don't take care of it here, ya can't be sure he won't buck ya off down the road. It might take a lot of time, but it won't be time wasted."

I had never done any roping and was reluctant to start something that I might make a mess off. But I knew the old men where the smartest I knew when it came to horses and I figured they knew what they were talking about. Amos lent me an old rawhide lariat. He showed me how to make a loop, throw a loop and recoil my rope quickly. I practiced a lot before trying it out on Bosco because I knew with his sensitivity he would not be very forgiving of my clumsiness.

After a few days practice Amos said I was ready. He suggested I just saddle Bosco first and let him go through his tantrum then I should rope the saddle horn and start with that. Well, it did not go very smoothly. Bosco bucked with just the saddle and bucked more when I roped the horn and pulled on it. When he finally settled from that episode I tried pulling on the stirrup. He was nervous and ran faster, but did not buck. But the worse was after he got good about the stirrup and I pull on the rope attached to the rear cinch. He nearly cleared the fence and roared louder than ever before. This horse carried so much anxiety and fear about these things I was feeling I was tackling something I was not nearly good enough to handle.

With Walt and Amos supporting me, I repeated the process for nearly two weeks. There was some improvement and even some really good days, but even after two weeks Bosco was not making sufficient change to consider him safe to ride. He was still nervous when the saddle was put on even if he didn't buck. Sometimes, he seemed to be doing great until ten minutes after he was saddled when he would spontaneously explode – which was a lesson in itself about how little progress in his feelings I had really made. Finally, I went to Walt and Amos again to admit defeat.

"Well matey, I can see ya problem and it ain't ya fault. And it ain't the horse's fault. But I think it's time now to force him to make a change. It's been goin on too long and I fear maybe some of his fear is a habit. I'm goin to show ya somethin that I hope ya will never need to use again in ya life. It's called a "runnin W" and been used by some to make a horse fall down. But we ain't goin to make Bosco fall down. We're goin to help him break a pattern. But first ya need to teach him to long rein."

With Walt's help I started the next day teaching Bosco to long rein. I know long reining is something that most trainers do, but Walt and Amos never did it; and for good reason – but I won't go into that here. Anyhow, I knew that for Walt to be teaching me to long rein that he must have thought Bosco was a special case. It only took about 3 days before Bosco

PICKINESS

was working well enough in long reins to go onto the next stage in Walt's estimation.

He showed me how to rig up a running 'w'. It involved a hobble strap around one front pastern, the lariat rope and the long reins. The idea is that when the lariat rope is tightened it pulls on the hobble strap and the horse lifts his foot off the ground. We started at a stand still. I pulled on the lariat, which caused Bosco to surge forward. As his foot came off the ground I shortened the rope, which stopped him from putting the foot back on the ground. He hopped a couple of circles before stopping again. I repeated this again and again until Bosco lifted his foot without fuss and without trying to walk away.

When that was looking good I repeated the whole process, but now I drove Bosco around the pen in the long reins. At first it was just at a walk. He was very quick to catch on and came to an immediate stop when I pulled on the lariat. Pretty soon I was able to ask him to trot, but this time there was far more resistance. I worked on this until he got the picture.

The next day I began where I left off and within thirty minutes I was able to ask Bosco to come to an instant stop from a canter. I then took him out of the pen and long reined him all over the property using the lariat to stop him from his front foot. After about another three days it was time to reintroduce the idea of wearing the saddle again. When I laid it over his back I felt his tension. I immediately pulled on the lariat to lift his foot. Bosco's back lifted and I was sure he was going to leap away and buck, but I held his foot off the ground. Maybe a minute had passed before I could visibly see the tension melt away. I fixed the cinches snugly and attached the breast collar. Again, I used the lariat when I saw him fixate on his troubles. He hadn't moved a muscle, but I waited and waited until eventually he relaxed and I allowed his foot back on the ground.

When all was set I asked Bosco to move off. Within two steps he humped up and leapt forward. I pulled his foot away and he tried to buck on three legs. But he must have moved only about four jumps before he stood there with a look of "what just happen?" on his face. He was shaking, but not moving. I waited until he stopped shaking before giving his foot back. I asked him to move again, but this time he was stuck. I guess he thought if he moved he would lose his foot again. Walt told me to keep asking and wait. Soon he tried a step or two and then another step or two. He started to tentatively walk with no buck. After a minute or two he was walking with a lot more confidence and looking relaxed.

This process was repeated over a few more days until Bosco was freely trotting and cantering with no sign of a buck. And if he did get worried it was enough to just put a feel on the lariat to calm him. When it came time to ride Bosco, I kept the lariat in my hand just in case. I did use it a couple of times, but after about three rides I abandoned the device altogether. To my knowledge he never did buck again.

Bosco was a rare horse with a problem that most trainers only see maybe once every few hundred horses. I have only ever used the "running W" on one other horse in my entire career. A better horseman may not have needed to use it at all. But I want to make the point that while contraptions like the "running W" were designed to cruelly force a horse to fall down, they can be used in ways that help a horse and cut through the layers of bad feelings that some horses build between them and us. Few horses will ever need something as invasive as a "running W", but if they do they don't have to be used brutally.

RUSTY AND ME

Sometimes we get a horse sent to us for training that is so fried that everything worries him. He stresses about everything in his life. Horses like this often spend large portions of their day frantically searching for something that will make them feel safe, but rarely find it. They are the horses that run up and down a fence line forming deep trenches. They sometimes stand in the corner of a yard weaving back and forth. Or they regularly run bucking and screaming in their paddock from some unseen, mysterious ghost. Horses like these are stressed to a degree it is hard to imagine. One such horse was given to me to work by Walt. The old man had purchased him at an auction with the intent of re-educating and selling for a profit. They often did this. It was a way for Walt and Amos to make a few dollars and afford the little luxuries of life like bread and tea.

The horse was an ex-racehorse who had only a few trials. From the start it was obvious that he was better suited to racing against one-legged little old ladies and the trainer sacked him even before he got to a race. When he arrived he came off the old truck like a red dragon breathing fire. He was 15.3hh and a deep chestnut colour. Amos pronounced his new name to be Rusty.

Walt turned to me and said, "Matey meet ya new mate. He's a little bothered 'cause it's his first day at camp. But I want ya to show him 'round and get him use to everythin. I know ya'll get along good and be great mates."

I took the lead rope and walked Rusty towards his yard. Well to be honest, Rusty pranced and I got dragged along with him. I discovered he was a bit head shy when I tried to take his halter off. But after a short struggle, Rusty was free to explore his new home. I left him alone for a while, but returned a couple of hours later to give him his nightly feed and check his water.

As Rusty saw me walk towards his yard he made an approach towards the gate. I guessed he knew what a feed bucket looked like. But when I unlatched the gate and entered he spun and headed to the far end of the yard in a dust cloud. He was on full alert with his head skyward, ears pricked, tail almost vertical and steam blowing with jet force through his nostrils. I decided to ignore his antics and go about my business as if he wasn't there. After I left the yard, Rusty left the far corner and investigated the feed bin. I figured he was going to work this out by himself so I left to finish my other jobs before going home.

The following day Rusty was just as nervous and wary about getting close. His fear was bleeding all over the yard. He kept away from me as I fed and cleaned his yard. When I tried to approach him to stroke his shoulder he scooted out of the corner at lightning speed. He was careful not to run me over, but his fear was obvious. Walt and Amos were in no hurry for me to being working with Rusty, so I decided to just be laid back about the whole thing and go about my business without pushing myself onto him.

Within a few days Rusty was becoming far more curious about me and it seemed he was beginning to believe that I posed no threat to him. I could now touch him and he even started to eat a little grain from my hand. After a couple of weeks of Rusty arriving he was greeting me at the gate and following me around his yard. I decided it was time to halter him and start his training. Because he was head shy I could only get a halter on him if I unbuckled all the straps and fit it down low on his neck, then gradually slide it up his neck before buckling the nose strap. Once the halter was fitted he was pretty good about being touched – even around his ears. But taking the halter on and off was a project I needed to devote some time towards.

Each day I tried to spend at least some time with Rusty. Walt was proving to be right when he said that Rusty and I would become good mates. Over the weeks his haltering was improving along with a slew of other problem areas like picking up his feet, leading and bending. One thing I noticed was how much more closely he was paying attention to me. He didn't seem to be so easily distracted by other things happening around him like other horses calling or a sheep moving in a shadow. I thought all this was looking much better. But I did notice that when I let him go back in his yard he would run and call out again. He was always unsettled for some time after I gave him his freedom back. When I walked back to his yard he would settle again. This happened when I tied him up somewhere too. If I tied him in the wash bay he was fine while I was nearby. But if I walked out of sight he would start to fidget and after a few minutes be would become frantic. I reckoned it was a good thing that he got so much confidence with me close by, but it worried me that he was so worried when I wasn't within sight.

"Walt, what do you make of it?" I asked.

"Well matey, ya doin a good job. Rusty is gettin better all the time and he sure thinks ya the bees knees."

"But Walt, should I be worried that he loses the plot sometimes when I go away?"

"Matey, when Amos and me were young – maybe twelve or thirteen – our mum and dad decided we had enough schoolin and we needed to bring in some money. It was depression days and people didn't have much. There weren't no work in the city, so we packed our bags and mum put us on the train to Tingha were dad had fixed up a job with a drover for us. It was our first time away from home and our first job. The bloke we worked for was a gruff ol' fella, but he was kind in his way. As long as we didn't talk back and put in a days work he treated us fair.

"It was hard work and more than once Amos and me thought about packin it in. But it seemed that as long as we had each other we were okay and we could send a coupla bob home to mum every fortnight. After a while keepin them horses fed and shod, makin camp and cookin the meals, as well as mindin the sheep, was all we had time to think about. We settled into life on the long paddock.

"Then one day Amos got real crook. The boss said it was appendicitis and we needed to get him to a doctor. I had to stay with the sheep and the boss took Amos to town. When the boss got back there was no Amos. At first I thought he might've died, but the boss said he was in hospital and would have to stay for a week. The next day we packed up the camp and moved on. The boss said we'd pick Amos up on the way back through town. With Amos gone I had more work to do, but the boss took a bigger load too. I began to fret with Amos not bein there. He was me brother and a right pain he could be, but we were never apart and havin him there made things easier. But now he was gone and I became more scared. I worried about doin the wrong thing and the boss yellin at me. I worried about the horses chuckin their hobbles and gettin away in the night. I worried about gettin to a dam before the sheep died in the heat. I didn't worry about any of these things when Amos was there, but now I worried about everythin. It was me first job and Amos wasn't there to back me up.

"When we finally went through town again, Amos was stayin with a friend of the boss. He had been eatin like a king and playin with the other kids. But he told me that he wasn't happy there 'cause he kept worryin about me, about doin the wrong thing, about mum and dad. He couldn't be happy in paradise. Now that we were together again, everythin began to feel okay. We finished the drovin season with no problem.

"The next year Amos and me couldn't get jobs with the same drover, so we had to split up. It was hard at first, but because we had learned the ropes and knew our job it was a lot easier than the year before. We missed each other, but knowin how to be drovers and seein familiar people from last year meant we were a lot less stressed and soon found the work to be good. The things that worried us and had us frettin when we were pulled apart a year ago weren't no longer any problem. We were seasoned drovers by now and didn't need each other to make us feel safe. D'ya get what I'm sayin matey?"

I looked at Walt blankly for a moment before speaking.

"I think so. Your saying that Rusty gets comfort from me and so feels better when he is with me than when he isn't. But once he gets better with knowing his job and feels okay about it, he won't be depending on me so much."

"That's right matey. He'll get confidence in himself knowin what's expected. But he has to go through this worry first. A horse learns to first have confidence in his environment, his home. Then he develops confidence in the routine of his handler or his job. Finally, if he's lucky, he learns to have confidence in himself. He figures out that he can handle any trouble without the help of a mentor or familiarity of his surroundings. Most horses learn to be okay with their environment. Most learn to be okay with their job or mate (even if they don't feel good about it). But only a few ever get to have self-confidence in strange situations. But if ya handle it right matey, Rusty might make one of those few one day.

A HORSE'S LIMITATIONS ARE OUR LIMITATIONS

"Hey Ross," it was the boss calling out to me from across the yard. "Would ya be interested in helping out with working a horse for Jerry? Jerry, this is Ross the young fella I've been telling ya about."

The boss introduced me to his friend Jerry - a man with greying hair in his mid fifties. He had the look of somebody who spent a lifetime in the sun and had worked hard every day of it. I felt small when we shook and he engulfed my young hand.

"Jerry has a seven-year-old Warmblood gelding that needs some work," the boss said.

"I've got to go away on business for a few weeks and I need somebody to put some time into him otherwise he will be feral when I get back," Jerry explained.

"Well what sort of work do you want done?" I asked.

"Just ride him in the round yard. He's pretty green and I haven't taken him out of the round yard yet since I broke him in. He's a nervous type and gets spooked by things and he's really scared of cattle. But I think you'll like him. He tries really hard, but he can be lazy like a lot of Warmbloods. I've been working on his "go" button, but it needs more work," Jerry added. I was getting mixed signals about what this horse was really like.

I had to ask, "Do you reckon he is ready to be ridden out of the round yard yet?"

"Well, maybe. I think you should ride him in the round yard for the first few rides and see if you think he is ready."

This led me to my next question. "How much work has your horse had?"

""Oh I dunno. I broke him in just after turning 3 and he probably averages 3 or 4 rides a week," Jerry said.

"What?" I thought. This horse has been ridden 3 or 4 times a week for 4 years and he has never been outside the round yard! What did this fellow think he was doing?

We agreed on a fee and I said I would begin working with Rocket the next weekend. I had my reservations because I wondered how bad must this horse be to ride if he is not safe to take out of a round yard for 4 years! But I was actually pretty excited about my new project. It was always exciting to start with a new horse. Besides this was the first horse I was given to train that hadn't come from Walt and Amos. I guess I was starting to make a name for myself.

My first session made me realize that calling this horse Rocket was either a joke or wishful thinking. He was duller to the leg than any horse I had ridden. A dead horse would have more reaction to being asked to go. This was accompanied by no response whatsoever to the reins. It was like riding a rock rather than a rock-et. This was not laziness. Even riding with a crop did little more than elicit a jog from him. Rocket was so completely shut down that hardly anything made an impression on him.

After the session I went to find Walt and Amos. It wasn't hard because they were sitting under their favourite tree eating a sandwich and drinking a cup of tea from a thermos that looked like it had been left to them by a first fleeter from 1778. They had been watching the whole time.

"Well matey, I can't disagree with ya. That horse is badly shut down and puttin a whole lot of effort into tryin to ignore ya," Walt said.

"Well, what should I do?" was the obvious question.

"I think ya gotta get him out of that round yard. He is goin to struggle to wake up while he is in the same routine. Ya gonna have to change his pattern and put him in situations that are gonna challenge him."

A HORSE'S LIMITATIONS ARE OUR LIMITATIONS

"Jerry said he is afraid of cattle. Maybe we could take him down to Mr Mosley's at the end of the road and use his steers," I suggested.

"Yeah matey, we could do that. But first maybe ya should just ride him in the arena, then the paddock. Try and get a handle on gettin him to listen to them reins and legs first before ya put him in a scary spot. There's every chance that when Rocket wakes up it's goin to be badly troublin to him. Ya might want to have some response to them reins before that happens," Amos added.

The next session I started doing groundwork in the arena. I had never seen a horse put so much effort into putting out so little effort. He was working just as hard at tuning me out as I was at trying to get him to listen. I thought he could be a fun horse if I could only channel that same amount of effort into activity rather than inactivity.

I decided to lunge Rocket and try to really put some pressure on him to provoke him into doing something different other than just plodding around the circle. I found an old plastic chaff bag and held it in my free hand as I asked Rocket to circle around me. Three or four times I asked him to trot and three or four times it was like knocking on the door of somebody who isn't home. So I lifted my hand with the chaff bag and had a fit. I waved that bag like it was caught in a tornado. I stomped my feet and charged at Rocket's girth flapping for all I could. Halleluiah!! I got him to jog. Now any other horse would have run for the coastline with the amount of energy I had just erupted with, but Rocket jogged. I was mad. What was wrong with this stupid horse? I decided to do it again until he cantered. Just as I was about explode again I was stopped in my tracks.

"Now wait a minute matey. Go and pet him." I hadn't seen Amos standing in the shadow of the tree. "Go on. Pet him"

"But Amos..." I started.

"No buts. He did what ya asked. He made a change. He made a try. And ya want to go and get him a whole heap of more trouble because ya think he should have given ya more. Well ain't you a greedy bloke? He just gave ya everythin he had and ya still want more. Now pet him and do it agin."

I did what Amos said and the result wasn't much different. But Amos told me to repeat it and repeat it. By about the sixth or seventh time I repeated the exercise Rocket started trotting before I blew up. It was a change.

"Now ya better ride 'im before ya wear him out."

I did as Amos told me while he coached me through the process of convincing Rocket that putting an effort into his walk and his trot was a good idea. It was Rocket's first ride ever out of the round yard in his four years under saddle. Even though he seemed a little more awake than his ride in the round yard, his interest was in the things around us and not in listening to me. Amos helped me make a change. We got him to trot from a big bump with my leg, then from a small bump with my leg and finally from just my seat. It was a good place to stop and to build on during the next session.

"Tomorrow matey, I reckon it would be a good idea if ya ride in the jump paddock. He'll be okay. He might have a hard look at some of them jumps, but I don't think he will do anythin. He needs a place to go to and he ain't findin it when the fences close in on 'im."

The next session began in the jump paddock. I started with lunging him and was pleased that he was a lot more responsive to going forward. I only had to use the chaff bag a couple of times. Amos and Walt were both there to keep an eye on proceedings. I could see from the look Amos gave me that he was pretty happy with the change in Rocket. It was time to ride again.

I was able to get a better walk out of Rocket. I showed him all the coloured poles and dazzle boards, but they hardly registered on Rocket's radar. When I asked for a trot with my legs I don't think Rocket heard me, but when I yelled for a trot with my legs he made a fairly abrupt transition. I let him trot for a few metres and then walk and tried the transition again. He was right there and listening. What a change from the day before. I did a few more transitions and he was getting better with each attempt.

I decided to ask Rocket for changes in his rhythm. We trotted around a few jumps and then I asked him for more response in his forward. As I asked him to get more life I felt him sucking back and slowing up. I tried to urge him forward with effort from my seat and legs, but he stopped and humped up. He didn't buck, but I felt one was there. I heard Amos' voice.

A HORSE'S LIMITATIONS ARE OUR LIMITATIONS

"Just pet on him matey and don't ask him to go." I did as Amos told me and I felt Rocket relax.

"Pick up ya left rein and bend him this way and let him walk over here," Amos was saying.

When I reached the old men I asked what had happened.

"Well, I think he is afraid to go," Walt piped in. "It seems that puttin out an effort scares him. The more you push him the more worried he gets. If ya had pushed 'im too hard ya ride might 'ave been a tad more excitin for a few moments."

"What should I do now?" I asked.

"Ya just hang on there matey for a minute. I'm goin to get Cally saddled and I will come and help ya." Amos walked off to get his horse.

When he came back riding Calico he asked Walt to halter Rocket and hand him the lead rope. He ponied Rocket and me all around the paddock while I just sat in the saddle and rubbed his wither. He told me not to use the reins or my legs, but just enjoy the ride. After walking for a few minutes Amos trotted his horse and Rocket came along. It was a just a jog to start with, but over the course of a lap around the paddock Amos trotted fast and bigger. Rocket was a little worried at first, but I sat quietly just rubbing and talking to him. It wasn't long before we were striding out with an amazing amount of effort from Rocket. It was time to go to the next step. Amos told me that he would lead Rocket, but I was to ask him to trot. If Rocket held back Amos was going to trot Calico out with life to encourage Rocket to put out an effort. The first time we did it Rocket got stuck and when Calico trotted Rocket almost reared before coming forward. I did my best to pretend it didn't worry me, but I knew I was rubbing Rocket's wither a lot harder and it wouldn't have surprised me to discovered he was going to have a bald wither by the end of this ride. Amos repeated the exercise again and again. It took about four tries before Rocket was trotting off just from my leg. Next I asked him to trot bigger from my leg. When I felt him think about holding back, Amos sent Calico forward and Rocket along with him. It was great. Pretty soon I was able to get Rocket to trot fast and slow just from seat and Amos was only there for support. We were all really proud of Rocket and the changes he was making.

"Tomorrow matey, we will do this again, but without the lead rope. I'll ride Cally here with ya, but only as support. Ya'll do all the directin. Who knows we might even get a canter."

The next day didn't start out as well as we had hoped. Rocket didn't listen to my leg at first and Amos had to pony him forward for a few transitions before I tied the lead rope around Rocket's neck and rode solo. Amos kept close with Calico, but I was doing all the directing on Rocket. Walt was sitting on an old chair in the shade of an overhanging gum tree just inside the gate. As we rode past Walt suggested it might be time to see if Rocket would canter.

Amos told me to build the trot to be bigger and bigger until I felt he was almost ready to fall into a canter, then bring him back to a normal rhythm trot. I did this, but the first couple of times I felt him holding back and thinking about a buck as we got close to warp speed. Rocket just couldn't take himself to letting go enough to approach the canter. He was getting worried again and I could feel I was losing my throttle again even at a slower rhythm.

"Don't worry matey, I'll help ya," said Amos. "I'm going to trot ahead around the paddock and I want ya to just keep him trottin followin the fence. When I start comin up behind ya I want ya to urge Rocket to go with me and Cally. As I get along side I want ya to do ya best to stay with us for a few strides and then I'll slow up and ya bring Rocket back to a walk. I reckon a few times of that will help him think more forward. We'll give it a go and see eh?"

Amos took Calico ahead and I asked Rocket to just trot. He was not nearly as forward as before, but I didn't push it and accepted the piddly trot he was offering. I saw Amos coming around the top end of the paddock and knew he would soon be catching up to us. A minute or so later I heard the sound of Calico's feet and breathing approaching from behind. Shortly after that Amos shouted to me to push Rocket a little more. I felt Rocket surge forward at the sound of Calico getting closer. Then I realized that Amos had taken his horse into a canter and they were closing the gap pretty quickly. A few seconds later Amos was along side and going ahead. Just then he said, "Ok matey, time to put a little pressure on him."

A HORSE'S LIMITATIONS ARE OUR LIMITATIONS

At that moment I applied a small amount of leg pressure and I clucked with my tongue. Suddenly Rocket came alive and lived up to his name. He leapt forward with his front feet off the ground and I got thrown back into the saddle. In two strides we went past Amos and Calico as if they were standing still. Rocket was bolting and I couldn't hold him. Later Walt told me he had never seen anybody whose eyes were as large as mine when Rocket jumped in the air.

Rocket had taken off and there was nothing I could do except either bail or hang on. We were heading as fast as he could go towards the gate. I tried to turn him away from the gate in the hope that he would run himself out. But nothing was changing his mind. It was clear that Rocket was charging for the gate and nothing could be done about it. It was then that I noticed Walt leap out of his chair and take off running with the agility of a squirrel monkey.

I knew Rocket was going to either stop at the gate or try to jump the gate. I tried to prepare myself for both knowing that either choice could be bad for us. About two strides from the gate I felt Rocket prepare to stop and braced myself for the collision. He hit the gate with a thud and bounced back of it almost stumbling onto his rear – but he didn't. He stood there, sweating, puffing and a little dazed. I sat there for a moment and began to laugh.

Walt came running up to me shouting with an anger I had never heard before.

"Don't you ever, ever do that again." He got a fright. He was scared that something bad might have happened to me. I told him I didn't know he could move so fast, but he walked away furious and cursing at me, Amos and everybody else in the world and their mothers.

Amos rode up and checked we were okay. Then he surprised me.

"Tomorrow, this fella will be a different horse. Go put him away, matey."

He was right. The next ride was in the arena and Rocket was the best I ever felt. I even got a couple of canter transitions with only a very minor worry to them. I started taking him on trail rides and he was even a little rushy. It took nothing for him to listen to my seat and legs on the trail. Then with the help of Amos I took Rocket to the neighbour's property

129

and taught him to track and direct cows. At first he was very scared of the beasts, but when he learned that he could move them he really began to get into it and enjoyed pushing the cows through gates and around barrels.

As Rocket's forward response improved, so did his softness to the reins. He was one of the first horses that you could feel soften through his whole body. It was an amazing and memorable experience. Before Jerry came back from his trip, Amos rode Rocket in the arena and explained to me about how a horse uses himself when he is correct. It still stands out in my mind as a turning point in my understanding of correctness. Amos was riding Rocket like they were part of each other. I never saw him do anything, but Rocket did everything from an extended trot to a collected canter. It was an amazing thing to watch.

I asked Amos why the day Rocket bolted in the paddock changed everything for him.

"Well matey, Rocket was gettin better, but he was still shut down. The wall he had put up to protect himself from being nagged to death by people had a few more holes in it, but it was basically still a fairly solid wall. The reason he bolted was because the solid wall fell down. All that stress and anxiety he used to keep the wall in place crumbled in one moment. It was the moment Cally cantered past and ya told Rocket to go with him. Rocket suddenly woke up and got scared. More scared than he had ever been n his life. He didn't know what to do, so he took off. But when it was over, it was over and the wall was just a pile of rubble. Then he became available to have a conversation. The wall weren't there to block what ya had to say anymore. Do ya get it, matey?"

I'm not sure I did, but I knew Amos was right.

Jerry and his daughter came out to watch me working Rocket before taking him. Jerry was very surprised to see me saddle the horse in the arena. I hopped on and rode around at all the paces and even did a crude shoulder-in. We opened the gate and I rode all around the property. We opened and closed gates into paddocks, rode between cars and floats, rode through the stable barn cantered down the driveway, out the front gate and down the rode as a car flew past. Jerry and his daughter followed to watch as I trotted past Mr Mosely's steers with no problem. Rocket

A HORSE'S LIMITATIONS ARE OUR LIMITATIONS

was the perfect horse in everything we did. I asked Jerry if he wanted to ride Rocket back to the riding school, but he said he didn't bring the right boots. His daughter said that she would like to ride him back, but Jerry said that it was not a good idea since she had only ever ridden the horse in a round yard. I was a little disappointed that they didn't ride, but that was their choice.

As I was unsaddling Rocket I overheard Jerry telling the boss that he thought I had done a good job.

"The kid did fine. I mean I would have preferred if Amos or Walt had worked the horse. I had my doubts when they said to ask the kid. But I think he did okay."

They took Rocket home and I figured I would never see him again. But about three years later I had a reason to visit their property with the boss. We were there to pick up some hay the boss had bought from Jerry. The daughter met us in the front yard and my first question was to ask how Rocket was going.

"He's great. Dad thinks he is going really well. He's down the yards at the back riding him now if you want to go and see him."

I wandered down the hill and saw Jerry riding Rocket in a round yard. The horse was jogging along over bent with his tail swishing like it was the worst fly season ever. I said hello and listened to Jerry tell me how great Rocket was going. He showed me what he called a collected trot, shoulder in, half pass, passage and piaffe. Rocket was crooked, none of it was true collection, and none of it had impulsion. I asked if he had been trail riding him. Jerry said that he hadn't because Rocket had never got over his spookiness and was still too green to be trusted outside of the round yard. He even had to keep Rocket in a stable all the time because the neighbour would graze his heifers in a paddock right next to the only paddock they had for Rocket. Jerry looked at me as if to say "of course you know how bad Rocket is about cows." My only thought was that it was just too sad.

THE ART OF COMMUNICATION

Every riding school or boarding property has them. They are as much a part of these establishments as manure piles and weeds in the paddocks. They are constant and part of the landscape. I'm talking about a clique of teenage girls. The members of the clique come and go, but the group is ever-present. There is always a Queen and each member yearns to be her best friend. But even more than that, they all dream of the day when the Queen moves on and they become the new high priestess.

The riding school where I worked was no exception. At the time this story is placed Bobbie was the tribal priestess. She was about fifteen and was revered by the others for her daring. She was the first of them to smoke and the first to shoplift from Mr Rigozza who owned the local corner store. But what really made her numero uno was that she was the first to have a cool boyfriend. Second in charge was Bobbie's older sister, Wendy. She was a year older, but not as bold or scandalous as Bobbie despite her desperation to be like her sister. Then there was Narelle and Sarah and poor Maria. Maria was only thirteen and so much wanted to be part of the group. She was often the butt of their jokes and was far too nice for the coven of witches. But they tolerated Maria for two reasons. Firstly, she was useful as a slave. But more importantly, Maria was striking to look at it and everyone knew that she was going to grow up to be drop dead gorgeous. The other girls sensed that one day it was going to be to their advantage to be a friend of Maria.

My position at the riding school afforded me a certain status. Even though I was a manure shoveler and didn't come from money like the members of the group, I did have a certain authority and could make life easy or difficult for anyone I chose. Bobbie discovered this early when I caught her sneaking a boy into the girls' bunkhouse one night during a camp. At first she was all belligerent and abusive, but that quickly changed when she realized that I had the power to decide whether or not to report the incident to her parents. Bobbie was never again rude to me and she was always very helpful when asked to do something.

I saw the group huddled together talking as I was wheeling a barrow of manure over towards the pile. I stopped and asked what was the conference about.

"We were talking about that new boarder, Marilyn," Bobbie said.

"Oh yeah. What about her?" I asked.

"Well she says she is a psychic and can communicate with the horses. So I asked her to talk to Tempest and she came up with amazing things," Bobbie answered.

"Like what?"

"One thing she said was that Tempest is sad because she left somebody behind four years ago and hasn't got over it. Marilyn said it was a person that Tempi really loved. She said that is why she is so nervous all the time. It's so spooky because it was four years ago that Tempi was brought over here from New Zealand. Marilyn couldn't have known that. I never told her. She's amazing!"

"Well she told me that Penny doesn't like being in the paddock next to the jumping paddock because she used to be a jumper and every time a horse knocks down a rail it reminds her how much that use to hurt her legs. So I'm going to ask Ben if I can swap paddocks with Phil's horse," Narelle piped up.

I left the girls to continue their diatribe and toe dipping into the spiritual world of animal communication. I had work to do and if I was going to help Amos with his new breaker I had to get moving.

After the session with Amos and his horse I asked him about Marilyn.

"Amos, do you believe people can talk to horses and horses talk back?"

THE ART OF COMMUNICATION

"Matey, you do it all the time."

"No, I mean is it possible that you can read their thoughts and have a conversation with them? Can they tell you things like if their leg hurts or if they had an accident when they were a foal or stuff like that?"

"Matey, 'ave you been talkin to Marilyn?"

"No, but Bobbie and the girls have. Bobbie said that Marilyn told her that Tempest was nervous because she was heart broken about leaving a person four years ago. And it was four years ago when Tempest came from New Zealand! How could she know that? How could Tempest have told her that?"

"Matey, my question is how can a horse count? The last I knew countin was human invention and horses didn't buy calendars."

I was struck by the obviousness of Amos' observation. How could Tempest know how long ago it was since she last saw her friend? How would Bobbie's horse know how long four years is?

"Matey, I don't know if there is such a thing as psychic communication with animals. I don't reckon there is, but that ain't the same as knowin. But if there was such a thing, so what? What good does it do Bobbie to know that about her horse. She's got problems with that horse because she ain't helped it feel any better about workin with her. It don't matter if it's because of somethin that happened four years ago or because of a drop in the stock market yesterday. Bobbie still ain't doin nothin to fix it. So big deal if Marilyn is right or wrong. The problem is still Bobbie's to solve and the cause don't matter a hoot. D'ya think Bobbie's dad is goin to track down Tempest's friend and re-unite them. Nah. Miss Queen Bee needs to stop lookin for others to blame and others to fix it."

"But Amos if a horse tells you the saddle is hurting or the horse in his paddock worries him or he is afraid of jumping, isn't that useful?" I questioned.

"Of course matey. But do ya really need a psychic to tell ya those things? What sort of horseman can't get that information for himself by watchin his horse?"

I guess you're right, Amos. When you explain it like that," I said.

"Matey, have ya seen Marilyn ride her horse? What did ya notice?"

"Well, I know her horse is not very forward. Most of the time she has to keep kicking him and he pins his ears in the canter transition every time," I told Amos.

"Do ya really think that if Marilyn could talk to her horse and she understood what her horse was sayin that she wouldn't be able to sort out that problem? What sort of communicator allows her horse to be so cranky? I know for sure matey that you could help that horse have the prettiest transitions and you ain't got that much goin on up in ya head to be communicatin with," Amos chuckled.

Despite Amos' backhanded compliment. I saw his point about Marilyn and the trouble inside her horse.

Since then I have met about six people claiming to be animal communicators. They have all been very nice and sincere people. And they have all had horses that were troubled in their work. I have not met one communicator who had a horse that was happy and settled in their life.

But for me the most potent reason not to get involved with psychic communicators was explained to me by Amos.

"Matey, this stuff maybe real or maybe not. It don't matter. But horses are not so complex. They are more amazin than any of us can appreciate, but they ain't beyond any of us to make a good fist of understandin. The psychic stuff and the need to make trainin and understandin horses somethin so mystical takes away from ordinary people the realization that we all have the ability to be good horse people. Talkin to horses with our minds makes bein a good horse person out of the reach of most people and leaves it to only them special people with special gifts. It ain't so and folk shouldn't be made to feel they haven't got what it takes to be amazin with horses just because they can't read their minds."

FEEDING TIME

When I was working at the riding school as a general dog's body one of the responsibilities that was given to me was to feed the horses. I usually enjoyed this job. It meant that I got to drive the four-wheeler, go around the entire property, chat to people who arrived early or left late and pat most of the horses. I was rarely rushed and the boss was normally too occupied elsewhere to be looking over my shoulder. I was good at it too. I took care to notice if a horse was lame or had any cuts or had pooped in his water or was off his feed. Lots of times I noticed little changes in behaviour that caught an oncoming colic early or when feeding out I picked up that the feed was spoiled. If the boss or an owner ever had a problem with a horse they would often ask me if I had detected anything different and I could always given an answer based on what I had seen. I never had to guess because I watched every horse that I fed. I knew when the electric fence was not working properly or when a horse had been chewing on a rail. I think the boss appreciated that I was conscientious enough to notice these things.

The other reason I was given the job of feeding was because hanging around Walt and Amos had ingrained into my brain the importance of not allowing horses to crowd you when you had a feed bucket in your hand. It was pretty common to see new boarders on the place trying to get their horses away from them if they were feeding. Some would resort to gate feeders so they would not have to go into the yard or paddock.

But the boss would always take them down because he hated the horses that would paw at his gates.

Lucy was new to the place. She had bought a thoroughbred from a trainer who called the horse Muggins. But Lucy changed the name to Mugsy. He had only had about four trials at the racetrack and was such a disaster that he was sacked from racing without further effort. From what I was told, it's not that he wasn't fast because he was. The problem was that he was a nut to handle. It took four men to load him into a barrier. When in there he would try to back out or rear or paw desperately. When the gates opened he always shot off to the left almost oblivious of the horses next to him. On the corners he would swing out so wide a couple of times he nearly ran into the railing. And jockeys could not hold him back. He was far too strong for most. In just a few short hit outs at the track his reputation was so notorious that it was difficult to find a jockey or track rider prepared to ride him. So Lucy bought him for $200.

When he first arrived Lucy kept him a private paddock and came every day to feed him. By all accounts he was pretty rude about the feed bucket and Lucy developed a brutal right cross from swinging the bucket at him so much. She then got the idea of using a gate feeder, but the boss soon put an end to that. The next thing she tried was to take a whip into the paddock with her to drive Mugsy away when he got too close. That worked well for a little while. But he became really reactive and would buck and rear vertically, then run flat out across his paddock and even sometimes slam into the fence with his chest. After he broke a railing, Lucy became really frightened that he would hurt himself or hurt her, so she asked if I would feed Mugsy during my usual rounds of feeding the other horses. She said it was because her work schedule had changed and she couldn't come to the paddock as often. But I detected she was getting afraid of him at feeding time. The boss said it was okay and he would add it to her account each month. It didn't worry me because I knew I had taught tougher horses than Mugsy to be polite about being fed.

The first time I went to feed Lucy's horse I decided to take a flag with me, but maybe not use it until I needed. I wanted to see how much Lucy had taught him and how reactive he was. When he saw me approaching his gate on the bike with the trailer towing behind he took off running laps in his paddock. He was jumping and kicking out as he ran like the grim reaper was chasing him. I watched for a moment or two before deciding that I should just dump the feed into his bin and leave him to sort it out. I trundled down the laneway to the next paddock with Mugsy still trying to flee the reaper.

He was the same for the next several days - always leaping and cartwheeling whenever I went to feed him. He didn't ever crowd me or threaten me and I never felt in jeopardy with his shenanigans. But I did feel sorry for a horse that was suffering that much inner turmoil. After about a week, Mugsy gave up tearing around the paddock. Instead he would stand off from his feed bin just rearing and cat leaping on the spot. He would fling his head violently then leap all four feet off the ground, spin around and double barrel out with his back legs before hitting the ground and then rear vertically. There was no doubt about it, Mugsy was an incredibly athletic horse – very troubled, but athletic!

This was about as good as his behaviour became. Even after several weeks he was never very settled when it came to feeding. He could be really good to handle and even his riding had made great progress. But at feed time all that would be forgotten.

Lucy asked to have him moved to a group paddock because her finances could no longer afford a private paddock. Mugsy was put in with four other horses. We picked the four most settled and quiet horses hoping they would be a good influence on him. At first this looked like a bad idea. Mugsy got picked on ceaselessly. One of the mares that was probably normally the quietest would charge Mugsy from halfway across the paddock, bum first with back legs firing. None of the horses would be his friend. Even though he was in a smallish paddock with four other horses, he was alone and isolated. I felt quite sorry for him.

At feeding time, Mugsy was chased far away from the others. I had to put his feed bin at the opposite end of the paddock to make sure he got to eat. When I walked the feed over to his bin he would still leap and rear as he followed me at a safe distance. It seemed nothing had changed. It was very peculiar and I had never seen a horse behave that way before.

"Ya wanna know why them horses ain't friends with Mugsy, matey?" Walt answered. "Just look at 'im. Look at the way he carries on. Would ya want to hang around somebody like that?

"Me and Amos had a cousin, Len. When we was all kids, Len's dad was a tough fella and he was toughest on Len. Poor kid could do nothin right and his old man was always criticisin 'im. When we was little we all played together, but as we got older Len started actin funny. He got sick a lot and acted sorta nervous. Things changed and we started not wantin to be around him 'cause he would do strange things, cruel things. Len grew up with no friends, never got married and lived alone his whole life. When he died it was only family that went to the funeral."

"Sounds to me, Walt, that there is a strong family resemblance," I said with my tongue in my cheek.

"Cute, matey. Very cute! But ya get my point, don't ya? Mugsy is so troubled that them other horses don't want him around. He upsets the balance of harmony they got worked out in the paddock. They feel better if Mugsy is off somewhere else instead of with them."

"Okay, but can that ever change, Walt?

"You bet. But it has to come from a change in how Mugsy behaves. It won't come from the horses. They might eventually get used to 'im and just accept that he's around, but he will always be an outsider until he behaves more like a normal horse. And that can only happen when he changes the way he feels and learns appropriate behaviour."

"So how can he do that?" I asked.

"Well take the feedin thing as an example. Since you're the one doin the feedin, have ya tried puttin a halter on him before you take in his feed bucket? Maybe lead him over to the bin and ask him to stand quietly a few feet away until ya dump the feed and let him off the halter. Anytime, he decides to get excited, shut him down. Tell him this ain't goin to work and teach him to walk with ya quietly and to wait until ya say it's okay to eat. Don't be lettin him carry on like a movie star whose bottled water is the wrong temperature. Interrupt that idea with ya lead rope. When he thinks about bein quiet, you be quiet too. It won't take more than a few days before a smart horse like Mugsy will be a pleasure to feed and ya won't need the halter and lead anymore.

FEEDING TIME

"But there's a lot more trouble inside that horse than ya goin to fix with the feedin problem. And that's goin to be Lucy's responsibility – not yours. So ya limited in how much you can do for Mugsy. But as he worries less and less about life, ya'll see he will start to make friends with some of them other horses. It might take awhile and it might not be real easy, but I know the horse doesn't need to be this way and don't want to be this way. He's a victim of what us two legged animals have done to him – just like cousin Len."

Walt was right. When the summer came, Lucy spent more time with Mugsy and even got some help from Walt. It was interesting to watch the changes come over the horse. Bit by bit he stopped his nervous behaviour. He may have taken 8 months or more before Mugsy became one of the herd and not just an intrusive visitor. Things all changed at the same time. Mugsy would met Lucy halfway to be caught, he was quiet to handle, could be tied up for hours without fussing, was a pleasure to feed, made a few friends in the paddock and learned to be a nice riding horse.

I think we often think that the horse we see in front of us is the horse that is there. But, like people, often what you see is not always what there is. The trouble our horses feel when we are with them can carry over to how they are in life, with or without us around. That trouble that we put in them can become a way of life and habitual behaviour sets in. We often think it is just the horse's nature and this is how he came out of his mother. But it's not always true. A horse's experience with humans can shape his whole attitude to life and not just affect his behaviour when we work with them.

THE ROUND YARD

Stella was a Paint mare Walt had picked up at an auction sale. She was about seven years old and Walt thought she had probably had at least one foal. He had bought her really cheap and had plans to work her to sell again. This is how the old brothers often supplemented their meagre incomes and they were good at it.

I use to feed Stella and clean her yard on weekends and got to like the mare. She was nervous of new things, but smart enough to quickly evaluate their danger to her or not. She had been at the riding school for about three weeks before Walt finally got around to deciding he had better put some time into her before she was no longer a cheap horse. He asked me if I would like to help with training Stella and I could not have been keener.

Walt told me to get Stella and take her into the round yard and we would start with seeing what was going on inside her. I haltered Stella and led her out of her yard. She was a bit pushy to lead and was trying to take me for a walk rather than the other way around. I finally got her into the round yard and waited for Walt to show up. Stella kept walking around me and was not in the least interested in my presence. Eventually Walt appeared and saw me holding a very fidgety horse.

"Well matey, what are ya goin to do with her now?" he asked.

"What do you want me to do, Walt?"

"Ya might start with gettin her feelin betta so she can pay attention to ya," he said. "Why don't ya take off that head collar and let her go for a bit?"

I removed the halter and Stella trotted to the opposite side of the yard closer to where she could see other horses. I looked at Walt as if to ask "now what".

"Now matey, take about three feet from the end of ya lead rope and whack the ground as hard as ya can. But don't try to drive her anywhere, just whack the ground. Maybe whack it behind ya so she don't think ya tryin to hit her."

I did as Walt told me, but nothing happened. Stella was too focussed on the other horses to notice.

"No matey, I mean whack it hard on the ground – hard enough to open up a crack in the earth."

I tried again. This time I gave it everything I had. Stella jumped and took off running around the track.

"Now stand there matey. Don't do anythin – just let her work this out," Walt ordered.

I stood there passively and watched Stella run several lapse around the pen. After about the fifth lap she suddenly stopped where she could see the other horses and then ran the other way. Another lap and she stopped again close to where the horses were. This time she stood looking out of the yard at the horses.

"Time to whack again, matey – but not so hard," Walt told me.

I whacked the ground behind me just enough to cause a tremor rather than a fully blown quake. Stella took off again in the pen. But this time after about the first lap she slowed down and finally stopped and looked at me.

"Now matey, don't do anythin just yet – just wait."

A minute or so went by. Stella looked back towards her horsey friends.

"Let her look for a bit, but if ya think she ain't goin to look back at ya, whack the ground again. But only half as much as last time," Walt suggested.

Stella did not check back with me after about half a minute. This time I gently whacked the side of my leg with the lead rope. Stella walked off about half a lap of the yard, stopped and looked at me. She only looked at me for a couple of seconds, but then sniffed the ground for a few seconds, then looked at me again. Then the little paint mare turned and walked the other way and stopped nearest to her friends. I just lifted the lead rope against my side and Stella walked around the yard until she was behind me. Then she stopped and squared up to me, looking at me with both eyes. One of the horses called and Stella looked that way for a second or two, then looked at me again and walked a step towards me.

"Ya doin great, matey. Now ya could go and pat her if ya wanted, but let's wait and see what she does next," I heard Walt suggest.

I must have stood there three minutes thinking nothing was going to change before I saw Stella shift her weight onto her rear end and take another two steps towards me. I waited some more to see how far I could take this. Eventually after another few minutes Stella tentatively walked towards me and stopped within patting distance. I raised my hand to pat her.

"Don't touch her, matey. Just stand there for a bit. I'll let ya know when to pat her."

I waited and I waited until eventually Walt gave me the ok to touch her.

The session went on for a little while longer and we built on liberty work to get it a little stronger and make a change in how Stella felt. After Stella was back in her own yard I set about picking Walt's brains about what we just did.

"Ya ask hard questions, matey. So much went on in that short time that ya could fill a book," Walt said.

"When Stella came into the yard she was all prancy and fussy. Then ya let her go and she went to the other side of the yard closer to them other horses. Why did she do that?"

"I guess she was nervous, Walt," I said.

"She did it matey, 'cause bein with you in that yard felt bad to her and bein nearer them other horses was a better choice to her. We needed to change that. We could 'ave put her back on the halter and made her do what we wanted, but that ain't goin to change how she feels inside so it was always goin to be a battle between her needs and our wants. The best result would be to change how she felt about our wants. Let her make the choice that bein with ya is a better deal than with them other horses. Let it be her choice, but let it be the choice we want too.

"When that mare got her attention fixed on them horses and not you, ya whacked the ground and gave her somethin else to think about. She ran, but ya didn't make her run 'cause ya did nothin more than if a tractor went by. Ya didn't chase her around to run. She ran until runnin no longer felt good to her. Then she stopped runnin and went back to payin attention to them horses. Ya whacked again and she thought that was not too good and left them horses again. This kept up until she worked out that when she was lookin at them horses, there was energy in the pen and when she slowed and checked in with ya it was all pretty quiet. Soon enough she thought she might try to stick near ya and see if it was a better choice. But ya never made anythin happen. Ya never ran her around and around until she was desperate to try anythin else – even bein with ya. She made all the choices. Ya just weighted them choices a little in favour of what ya wanted. Ya never once directed her to run or come to you or look at the horses. All ya did was give her a reason to keep searchin for somethin that was better than she was already offerin.

"It's the difference between makin a horse choose between somethin that is hard and somethin that is harder or choosin between somethin is easy and somethin that is just a little less easy. If you make what ya want the easy choice – so easy that he would even choose it with no help from you – then he will feel good about workin with ya. But if ya just make his choices between hard and harder nothin will feel ok to him – everythin he does is troublin in one way or another – and he gives you everythin you ask for with reluctance and resistance."

"But why did you tell me to wait before patting her, Walt? Shouldn't I have gone in and rewarded her with a pat as soon as possible?" I asked.

"Well matey, that mare made the choice to take a few steps towards you. She weren't sure, but she figured that nothin else was working too good so she would try checkin in with ya and see if that worked for her. When a horse is teeterin on the edge of what she should or should not do, don't rush in and do somethin that might get her thinkin she made the wrong decision. The mare weren't totally sure that bein with ya was a good idea. She needed time to get sure. Let her get secure with her idea. Don't invade her space. Wait until she is feelin better. If she had wanted ya in her face she would have come right up to ya instead of standin three feet away. But then somethin changed and she got sure. She looked at you with both eyes, her breathing slowed, her ears stopped twitching back and forth to them other horses and her weight got planted on her front. That's when I knew she was ready to accept ya in closer to pat her with a good feelin."

I got to spend more time with Walt and Stella and I learned a lot about allowing a horse to make the choices I would like them to choose rather than making them choose what I want. It's hard to keep clear and sometimes the constraints of training for the public limits how much time you can allow a horse to work things out without some stronger prompting. But Walt understood better than anybody I have known how a horse's feelings are connected to everything they do.

THE WORLD IS A BOX

"Me and Amos had a cousin that was in a car accident when she was about seventeen. Dora was her name. She had a lot of sistas, but Dora was easily the prettiest and brightest of 'em all. Dora died about twenty years ago. She got some sort a cancer, but I don't remember which."

Walt or Amos didn't talk much about family. Sometimes I wondered if they were found under a bush. I don't know why he was telling me about Dora now when I really wanted an answer to my problem.

I was breaking in a Connemara filly, called Connie. She was only about 13.3 hh, but very stout and could easily carry an adult. But Connie was particularly jittery. Everything new scared her. She didn't shy in a big way, but she was fast and a fellow could get whiplash when she did. I had been working with Connie for a couple of weeks and didn't seem to be making much of a dent in her nervous reactions. I had worked her with a flag over and over, but the next day it was like she had never seen it before. The bush by the laneway she walked past every day caused her to shy every time. She never seemed to get over having the rug thrown on her despite exposing her until I no longer had the strength to lift it anymore.

But what was really giving me a headache was trying to catch her. I would walk into her yard with the halter and lead rope and Connie would head for the furthest corner and turn her bum to me. I knew better than to go up to a horse with her hind end facing me, so I flicked the rope at her rear to let her know this was not acceptable. When I would do this she would mostly run to another corner or sometimes even run a lap or two around the yard. If she turned towards me I was generally able to carefully walk up to her and slip the halter on – although she was pretty touchy around her ears. But quite often she would stand in another corner with her tail towards me and I would pretty firmly let her know with the end of the rope that she had better have another thought about that. I had been taking this approach since I started working with Connie and for the most part I was having to do less and she was taking less time to face me, but I always had to do something. I never was able to enter the yard with Connie looking at me, waiting to be caught. She always started out turned away from me. I knew this wasn't okay, but I didn't know why she wasn't much better than she was.

Yet, in other aspects of the breaking in process she was doing great. After the first couple of saddlings she started to wear a saddle as calmly as she wore her tail. Her groundwork and level of responsiveness to the lead rope and my body language was terrific and put older horses to shame. The way in which she learned to yield to the reins really impressed me and I knew she was going to have a mouth far too soft for most adult riders let alone a child. But despite all this really good improvement there was an underlying nervousness that seemed to be impenetrable.

That was why I was leaning against the old Bedford truck while Walt started to ramble on about cousin Dora. I wanted to know why she was still hard to catch and what I should do about it. I wanted insight into what I was missing and clues on how to help Connie let go of her constant worry. But Walt seemed to think I really wanted to hear about the family history. In the back of my mind I sort of knew that Walt was not one to wax lyrically about days past, so I figured there was going to be a point to the story about cousin Dora and I would have to be patient until he got there.

"Dora used to baby sit for Amos and me when we were little and would always play games with us until it was time for bed. She was so full of life and I reckon she was me favourite of all me cousins.

"Well, after the car crash Dora weren't never the same. She was in hospital for months with brain damage. When she eventually was allowed home her world was real different. She was slower and it was hard to talk to her 'cause her mind would jump from one thing to another real quick. She'd be tellin ya about going for a swim and in mid sentence she would talk about one of the chooks that had gone broody. Ya couldn't keep up with where her mind would take her. As kids we thought it was funny, but I can see how poor Dora really struggled later in life to have a job or a fellow in her life.

"One of her strangest quirks that she got after the crash was how she saw things in life. She seem to measure everythin the same way, but different."

"What does that mean, Walt?" I asked.

"Well matey, I remember how Dora saw everythin as a box. It don't matter what it was. It was always some type of box. After the crash her mind seem to have her see the world and all the stuff in it as boxes. All different boxes, but still boxes. The doctors had a name for it, but I can't remember what they called it. She damaged a particular part of her brain that made this happen."

"I'm not sure I understand," I said.

"Matey, everything was a box. If Dora saw a house, it looked like a box. A car was a box on wheels. A person was a thin box on its side and with legs. A balloon was a box with all the corners cut off. She could only see the world in terms of boxes. We ain't never learned why she saw the world like that, but somehow she needed to define everythin in terms of somethin she knew and boxes was the shape she knew best of all."

"That's weird Walt."

"I know matey. It's very weird. But somehow the brain was tellin Dora somethin that was different from the rest of us. To Dora it made perfect sense, but because our brains don't see everythin as a box, it don't make no sense to us. It's like sayin a Frenchman is talkin crazy because he speaks a language that's different from us. Dora didn't know she saw things weird."

"But Walt what has Dora's problem got anything to do with Connie?" I asked.

"Connie is a little like Dora. She sees the world in a weird way too. Different from you and me. She sees everythin as somethin that might get her killed. When ya go into her yard to catch her she turns away from ya.

She ain't sure you don't mean trouble for her. If the fence wasn't there she might leave and go into the next yard. But the fence is there and stops her from getting far away from ya. So she turns her back to ya. She ain't bein rude. She ain't bein disrespectful. She's just bein afraid."

"I get that Walt. But how come she does it every time? When I do eventually catch her she should be learning that I am not going to kill her. I haven't done anything that would make her think she is in trouble. I catch her, I pat her and rub her. I lead her quietly. There's nothing to be afraid about. So why do I have to go through the same routine every day?" I asked.

"Two reasons. First, the routine she goes through every time you try to catch her has kept her alive so far. In her mind she has lived through every experience by doin what she has done. If she changes and does somethin different, the outcome might be worse. Ya know some footballers go through the same ritual every time before a game. They eat the same breakfast, wear the same socks and pet their dog the same way. If they changed, they might have a bad game."

"Okay, I see that. Connie thinks that turning away is keeping her safe in some way. Even though it doesn't make sense, in her mind she lived through it, so it makes sense to keep doing it. I see how that could be," I said. "What's the second reason?"

"The second reason is that you have convinced her that people are a raw deal."

"What? Why?" I asked.

"Well matey, she believes that lettin somebody approach her with a halter in their hand is probably not a good deal. So she turns away. Then just to prove she was right to think like that, ya flick the rope at her and scare her."

"But Walt I wasn't trying to scare. I just wanted her to realize that I didn't want her rear towards me, I wanted her to face me."

"I know matey, but that's your thinkin. Her thinkin is that you were threatenin her. She already has enough worry about ya walkin into that yard and then ya just prove to her that she should be worried because ya tried to attack her with the rope. Why would she ever trust ya and greet you when ya go to catch her?"

"I didn't realize Connie would feel that way. I thought she would learn that facing me was a safer option," I said.

"I know matey. But ya see if ya had grown up with Dora ya'd have realized that every body sees the world differently. Maybe ya need to think about how Connie sees it. She ain't wrong, just because she's sees it differently. Maybe ya might try to make it easier for her to face ya, instead of harder for her to turn away."

OLD DRESSAGE VERSUS NEW DRESSAGE

When I was a kid dressage was a mysterious world to me. I saw the videos of horses performing feats of magic with little or no input from their riders. I remember seeing *The Wonderful World Of Disney* on television and watching Alois Podhajsky (played by Robert Taylor) with the dancing white horses from the Spanish Riding School escape from the Nazis. I was so impressed by those white stallions prancing and dancing, flying through the air. And all the time the riders seemingly part of their horse. I wanted to ride like that. I wanted to ride horses like that. But I didn't know the first thing about dressage. How to teach a horse to perform dance-like movements was not something the old men had ever talked about. I knew they knew a lot about horses, but maybe dressage was just as mysterious to them as it was to me.

There was a fellow who came to the riding school each Sunday to teach a lady who owned a big thoroughbred gelding. The instructor had trained overseas, competed at national level and was a student of the national coach. It would be hard to find somebody in Australia with more credentials in dressage. When Helen said she didn't mind if watched her lessons I was very excited. I figured this was an opportunity to infiltrate the secret world of dressage and I wasn't going to miss it. I was going to watch as much as I could, as often as I could.

CHANGING THE TIDE

I worked really quickly to get the stables cleaned and the water buckets changed-over. I missed the first ten minutes of Helen's next lesson with the guru in jodhpurs and top boots. I had only seen Helen ride on the trail and this was the first time I saw her in the arena. Her horse, Herbie was bought as a schoolmaster that had taught many people about dressage and had even competed at Prix St. George level in his prime. But now at sixteen years of age he was happily mentoring an aspiring dressage queen.

"Let him stretch a bit more. Push him on and let him reach into the bit. That's better. Now slow the walk just a fraction – he's over reaching. Good. Much better. He'll keep his rhythm easier now."

Helen was doing her best to follow her instructor's orders and he seemed happy with the result. Herbie was politely doing his best.

The instructor asked Helen for some trot work. Herbie threw is head in the air through the transition and trotted then stretched forward. Helen stopped Herbie to try the transition again and this time it was much smoother.

"Ask him to come down a bit more – he's too stretched out. He needs to start working from behind and get off his forehand. Just a bit. More contact and ask him forward."

I was shortly interrupted by the boss who told me to stop slacking off and get the horses ready for the next group ride. Reluctantly, I slid off the fence and left Helen and her coach to continue their lesson.

Even though my tuition in dressage was cut short this time, I had plenty of other opportunities to observe and absorb the secrets. I even tried putting some of what I learned into practice with one of the riding school horses with mixed success.

Watching Helen's lessons and asking questions of her instructor convinced me that in order to get the school horses to be better riding horses I needed to teach them to accept the bit more. So many of these horses just hung on the end of the reins and stretched out as they trotted and cantered around. Helen's horse was rounding up and travelling on the bit like a dressage horse should. It was obvious what a little dressage education could do.

But my efforts with the school horses were not as successful as I had hoped. There were definitely some issues to sort through, but I was sure I was on the right path. I was particularly working on getting the horses to accept the contact and carry themselves without leaning on the reins. I wanted them to engage their hindquarters and work from behind. But I was finding it was no simple project. I thought about talking to Walt and Amos about it, but after one particular lesson where I was able to ask Helen's coach a few questions, a whole lot of confusion cleared up for me. He even offered to watch me ride a horse and give his advice for free. He said it was rare to find such a keen student and he wanted to encourage me as much as he could.

During my demonstration ride the instructor watched closely and made a few suggestions before he asked if he could ride the horse to show me what he meant.

"You are on the right track, but the horse is leaning on your leg and not going into the bit. I would be a little more insistent that he obeys your leg. Let me show you."

He rode the horse forward with leg and a tap of his whip while asking the horse to give to the bit with a contact.

"There. Ya see that? He came onto the bit and I released the reins. Now I'll ask again."

The horse started to round his neck and give to the reins. Every time the horse was asked forward he threw his head up, but the fellow increased the contact until the horse gave again and then offered a small release. This happened again and again and the horse appeared to keep bouncing between giving and leaning on the reins. But I could see the progress and how you could teach a horse to round up and eventually collect.

I continued to work on these things over the coming weeks and I watched as many lessons with Helen and her instructor as time permitted. Helen's horse was working more collected than the first lesson and I could see changes in how much better he travelled. But I noticed he was having more problems with the halt. Helen seemed to have to use far more aids to ask for the halt. Even though he would listen to the seat to stop, he no longer listened very well to the reins. I noticed the same thing with the school horses I was riding in this new way.

I was surprised that even though the horses would give to the bit and round themselves, they became heavier whenever I picked up the reins. I couldn't understand why. Another thing that surprised me was that I was losing the rein back. The horses became really heavy on the reins when asked to back up. This was incredibly curious to me. I thought I must have been doing something wrong because even though the horses were looking more and more like trained dressage mounts they were leaning more on the reins than any horse that Walt or Amos broke in. That seemed very strange to me. I was sure this was different from Disney's dancing white stallions.

Then the day came that I saw Helen's instructor ride Herbie. He gathered Herbie up and rode him forward. There was an immediate stiffness come over Herbie even though he rounded up.

"See how he is engaging his back and really using himself," the instructor asked?

"Yes, I see. He looks great," was Helen's answer.

But I was not so sure. I couldn't see it. What I saw was a very strong rider holding up a very heavy horse that was stiff through his body with no sign of softening or getting lighter in the hand. He was more forward than before, but there was a "runaway" feel about his forward that bothered me.

"Walt, I don't think I'm interested in dressage anymore. It's not like I thought it would be. I guess you can't believe everything you see on Disney."

"Matey, there's nothin wrong with dressage. In fact it's good for ya and ya horses. Every horse could benefit from a bit of dressage trainin in its life. Ya've just seen some bad dressage bein called dressage," was Walt's response.

"So what's the difference?" I asked.

"Good dressage is about softness and unity. It starts with gettin a horse feelin right inside. When his mind is right he'll give ya the roundin and the collectin. But ya mate with the top boots thinks dressage is about gettin the position of the head and the body right and hope it gets the mind right. It's goin about it the wrong way. Because the horse is stiff and resistin, tryin to force him to arch his neck and go forward is squashin him like a concertino between two opposite forces. It just causes him more bad feelins and tension. If he got young Herbie to feel better about them reins, Herbie would give through his whole body when a fella picked up a contact. But Herbie don't feel good. Them reins should be a comfort to a horse, but Herbie has learned that the reins are a hindrance to 'im. They are the cause of discomfort, not the reason for comfort. So Herbie does his best to get along with them reins pullin on his mouth by shuttin them out of his mind. He figures the only way to find some relief is to try to ignore them as much as he can."

"Is that why he is getting more heavy in the hand and stiff through his body?" I asked.

"Yep matey. By tryin to shut out the bad feelins of them reins Herbie becomes heavier and heavier and stiffer and stiffer. It's his anxiety that's causin it. Some people, like that instructor fella, try to fix the problem by usin the reins to make the horse look like he is better on the outside. Instead of fixin the anxiety inside the horse that is causin all the resistance. Instead, they try to make the outside look like the inside is okay. But that's just wall paperin over a wall that's crumblin. It's trainin a horse backwards. Ya don't train the horse to carry his head in position to get him feeling alright. Ya train him to feel alright so that he can carry himself how he should. He'll give ya what ya want when he feels okay. But ya can't make him carry himself right when he don't feel okay."

"Walt, why doesn't Helen's instructor know that? He's a famous rider and teacher. How come he's going at it back to front?" I asked

"That's a very good question, matey. It use to be that when ya trained a horse he would get a bit confused and anxious when he didn't know somethin. But ya worked him until he got better and he became soft and relaxed. Then ya'd go to the next level of trainin and teach him somethin new that was a bit more difficult. He'd be a little confused and anxious, but ya kept trainin at that level until he learned to be soft and relaxed. Then go to the next level of difficulty and so and so on. Ya wouldn't ask for harder stuff until ya had the horse soft and relaxed with what he was learnin right now. That way, horses became softer and more relaxed no matter what level of trainin they were at. If ya horse was not like that ya'd go back a step and get him better at the easier stuff before movin to the next stage again.

But these days it's seems to be different. Ya see it at the shows we've been takin ya to. I've watched them dressage people ridin horses and doin lots of fancy stuff. But where is the softness and relaxtion? It looks to me that nowadays it's all about makin a horse do the fancy stuff whether or not they do it with or without a fight. People usin tight nosebands, hard bits, ridin on curb bits, spurs, whips. It's all about makin a horse perform. Horses get heavier to ride, stiffer in their bodies and shut down. I dunno why it's change. I guess it might have somethin to do with the fact that it takes skill and commitment to train a horse to be soft and relaxed and still perform right. But it only takes equipment and strength to make it look like a horse is performin right."

TRAINING WITH INTENT

One of the things that interest me as a trainer and student of horse behaviour is in regard to how a horse understands what we want. I am always impressed at how so many of our horses fill in the gaps in the way we ask. It's as if they already know the answer before the question is completed.

I met a girl called Sarah while I was working at the riding school. Sarah was fifteen years old and only a year older than me. The moment I met her I knew something was not quite normal about her. Sarah was my first experience of some one with cerebral palsy. A few years beforehand Sarah's mum got her interested in horses as a sort of physical therapy. Sarah developed an immediate love of horses and soon had her own horse called Bonny.

Bonny was a great little mare and was always so patient and kind with Sarah's awkwardness. Every weekend Sarah's mum would bring her down to the riding school to ride Bonny. She would haul out a lightweight ramp from her van for Sarah to walk up while Bonny led along side and waited for Sarah to get herself organized to get on. It was really something to see and Sarah became one of the most popular kids around the place. Even the cool girls would talk to her. But what most interested me was how Bonny was so good under saddle.

Sarah was always having little spasms. Her muscles would spontaneously contract every few minutes. It would cause her left arm to curl, her neck would twist and when riding her legs would jerk backwards. Yet Bonny never reacted to these spasms. She would carry on with her job just as if Sarah was the quietest rider you could imagine possible. But that is not to say that Bonny was a dull horse - just the opposite in fact. Sarah could ask with hardly any movement and that little mare was right on the job. Her canter transitions were smooth. Her response to the reins was light and her focus on the task was unwavering. Bonny was a very well trained, nice horse and she and Sarah clearly had great communication between them.

But I was intrigued how such a responsive horse could still ignore Sarah's lapse of muscle control. How could Bonny be so responsive to the lightest leg aid or touch of the reins, yet be so unresponsive to Sarah's spasms? I mentioned this to Amos one day when we were watching Sarah riding in the arena.

"Well matey, that mare knows when Sarah is talking to her and when she ain't. That's all."

"But Amos, how can she know the difference?" I asked.

"Matey, when I was a kid my grandad got Parkinson disease. That's a sickness where ya nerves act all haywire and ya hands shake, ya voice is slurred and ya ain't got a whole lot of control over ya muscles. A bit like Walt is – only he ain't got Parkinson's disease. Well grandad was a pretty handy horseman in his day. By the time he was in his seventies that disease had a pretty good hold on him and he was not very strong. I remember seein him workin a young geldin not long before he died. He could hardly stand and was leanin on a stick with the lead rope in one hand.

"His hand shook so bad that the lead rope looked like it was doin the jitterbug. I watched that horse lead up to right where grandad wanted him. It took nothing for that horse to figure out where he was suppose to be in the middle of all that rope wigglin. He stood quietly while grandad fumbled with getting the saddle on the horse's back and snugging up the grith. The only trouble was that I couldn't tell when he was shakin the rope to tell the horse to move or he was just shakin because of the sickness. But ya know what matey, that horse knew. He stepped back when grandad asked as pretty as you could wish. All I could see was a whole lot of shakin and movin of the rope that didn't have any sense to it. But that geldin did exactly as grandad asked with no fuss or confusion. And it weren't no different when grandad rode the horse. Through all that activity of grandad's shakin and tremours that horse could sift through what had meanin and what didn't.

"It ain't no different with young Sarah and her mare. Sarah ain't the prettiest rider. She falls all over the saddle and her limbs can't stay still for more than a few seconds. But that horse has worked out the difference between what movement that she needs to listen to and the movement that she needs to ignore."

"But Amos, how can a horse do that? What tells the horse what is important and what isn't?"

"Well matey, it is ya intent."

"What do you mean intent, Amos?" I asked.

"Ya seen me ride my horse Cracker with a flag, ain't ya?" he asked.

""Yep."

"And ya seen me ride Cracker while I've been flaggin another horse around the round yard, ain't ya?"

"Yeah," I again responded.

"Well, how do ya expect Cracker knew the difference between when I was talkin to him with the flag and when I was talkin to the other horse? I was me intent. It was the way I focused me and the flag. It's the same for Sarah and Bonny and the same for grandad. A horse can separate ya intent by the way ya focus ya use of ya reins, ya legs or ya body."

"Are horses really clever enough to do that?" I asked sceptically.

"Matey, not only are they good at it, they are better at it than you or I. Ya don't believe me do ya? Have ya ever spoken to somebody on the phone and they answered all ya questions, but ya had a feelin they were distracted or had somethin else on their mind? That you was more involved in the conversation than they were? Ya couldn't see what they were doin or what they were lookin at, but ya knew that their focus was somewhere else. It's the same thing with a horse. They know when ya mean it and they know when ya don't."

Like most of my experiences with Walt and Amos, the conversation I had just had didn't have a lot of meaning to me at the time. I found Amos' observations interesting and kept looking for evidence of his theory. There is no doubt in my mind that he was right. Horses can discern intent. I have seen it enough times when two people use the same technique on the same horse and get different results. Horses know the difference in our intent.

It is also been my observation that some of the most effective horse riders have been people who have less than perfect technique. Most of us spend a lifetime learning to become better riders and for most of us this means riding in the perfect position and using the perfect aids with perfect timing. Yet, so many riders with good position and good technique have screwed up horses. Why is this? I believe it is because nobody is teaching the effectiveness of "intent". Consistency and intent beat technique and position every time. A horse can rise above the obstacle of a rider with less than perfect balance or understanding of the aids, if the rider is clear in what they are trying to achieve.

I am not suggesting for one second that learning to sit and ride better are not important and worthy goals. But I am suggesting that they might be secondary to being consistent and clear in your intent. Sarah and Amos' grandad proved that to me.

TRAINING AND CHOICES

Not long ago I was talking to a client about when we ride or train a horse the only change worth having is a change of thought and that comes about by a change in the way the horse feels. If you can't help a horse to feel okay about a task then you can't change the resistance he offers. A horse that feels okay is a horse that will work at trying to make the job easy. But a horse that holds onto ill feelings about a job will always hold onto some resistance. Just like people. If you hate your job you don't put in your best effort – you just do the minimum to keep the boss from bugging you.

The client asked an excellent question.

"What distinguishes to the horse when to change his feelings or when to just give in with no change of feelings?"

She mentioned a video she had seen recently where a trainer was talking about how to mount a horse safely. He flexed the horse's neck to the left as he climb on board to prevent the horse from walking away.

"The horse didn't walk away when the guy got on, but if the horse felt okay about being mounted why did he have to bend his head around?"

To my mind, the answer is that if you have to flex the neck around to make sure the horse does not move then he doesn't feel okay and you shouldn't be getting on. His mind has wandered off. Why would you get on a horse that has mentally left the scene? But flexing the neck can allow you to get on a horse that is not thinking about being there with you. It just makes it more difficult for him to move his feet, but his mind is still leaving. Flexing the neck probably did not get a change in the feelings or the thought of the horse, but applied enough braking power to prevent the feet from moving.

Walt and Amos had come home from the auction with a 7 year old Warmblood mare. She stood about 16.2hh and was a rich liver chestnut – beautiful colour. As she came off the back of the old Ford truck she was breathing fire. Her first thought was to escape and tried to run by Amos who was holding the lead rope. Before the mare even knew what had happened Amos had sent a lightning fast flick down the rope and it whacked her under the chin with a loud crack. It stopped her in her tracks. She suddenly stood 20hh and looked at Amos as if he was the Grim Reaper come to take her to the bowels of hell. He approached and stroked her and then led her quietly to a clean yard.

Willow was a pretty nice mare, but her past handling had left her afraid and in constant flight mode. Life had clearly not been kind to her. Walt had given her a few days to settle before starting her education. By all accounts she had been ridden and even competed in dressage, but the owners found that she had become aggressive and would kick and bite if things did not go her way. Apparently the owner was leading her from the shoulder one day and Willow cow-kicked her in the rear. The owner could not sit down for a week! That was the last straw and Willow ended up at the market.

Walt spent the first week teaching Willow to lead properly and to stay focused. She had the habit of doing what she thought the person wanted and then instantly switching off. There was no attempt to prepare for the next thing. Willow would go through the motions and then was mentally gone when she thought she had finished. Walt took it fairly slowly with her to make sure there was no confusion. The mare was smart enough to catch on really quickly, but her inability to stay focused was a problem. Walt said it was a defensive strategy she had learned. And in order to break it down he had become intolerant of her detachment. At first this led to some clouds of dust being kicked up, but as she came to understand the importance of Walt in her life the acrobatics diminished.

Walt told me that he was going to start her tying up training tomorrow because he was sure she was a puller. I had some experience with this before. I had a friend whose father considered himself a horse trainer and I had seen Mr Reinhardt teaching another horse to tie up. He used a neck collar made out of an old Hessian bag and tied the horse really short to a big snubbing post in his round yard. He had the horse tied both from the rope head collar and the neck collar. Mr Reinhardt left the horse to work it out. It didn't take more than a few seconds before the horse started to pull back. When he realized he was tied up the horse gave it everything he had to get free. He pulled back over and over again and got in a really sweaty state. I have to say it made me feel uncomfortable to watch. After a while the horse finally seemed to give up the whole idea of pulling. Then Mr Reinhardt walked back into the yard and started cracking a lunging whip around the horse to encourage him to pull some more. He explained that if the horse decided not to pull back even when he was afraid, he would be a good horse to tie up and leave anywhere, any time. The whip certainly got the horse to pull back some more even though I thought he had no energy left to pull. Mr Reinhardt kept walking around cracking the whip as the horse fought his restraint until the horse stopped pulling and had no more energy with which to fight. By all accounts the horse did become pretty reliable at being tied up.

So I was really interested to see how Walt was going to teach the horse to tie up.

Walt led Willow around the outside of the round yard. He only had a rope halter and a long rope about feet long. Walt wrapped the lead rope three times around the post at a little more than wither height. He gave the mare about two feet of rope with which to move around. Walt walked about twenty feet away from Willow, unfolded a chair and sat down with the tail end of the rope in his hand.

It didn't take long before Willow got a little fidgety and felt that there was no give in the rope. This caused her great concern and she pulled back with everything she had. But the rope was not tied hard and the three wraps around the post allowed the rope to slide. Willow had to pull hard to get the rope to slide, but her desperation was such that she made it look easy.

However, the look on Willow's face when she realized the rope had given was priceless. After she had pulled about twelve feet she stopped with a puzzled expression. Walt got out of his chair, led Willow back to her spot and shortened the rope again. In a few minutes Willow pulled again, but this time with less panic and she stopped after only about eight feet. Walt led her back and shortened the rope. It took even longer for Willow to pull hard. At first she gave the rope a few tugs and then came forward again. Already this was an improvement. But then she decided to test it properly again and pulled the rope around the post another eight feet. Walt repeated the same procedure. It took perhaps another five or six repetitions before Willow stood quietly for 20 minutes without even an attempt to pull back. Walt put her back in the yard.

Walt followed the tying up lesson with several other sessions. He tied her up in several different locations and taught her to yield her hindquarters around if she wanted to look at something rather than just to pull back. Willow became a very reliable horse to tie up in time.

I was interested in the difference between the way Mr Reinhardt trained his horse and what Walt did with Willow.

"From most people's point of view there probably ain't much difference. But from the horse's point of view it's a world of difference."

"How so, Walt?"

"Well, when ya tell a horse he ain't got no choice in somethin, he makes no change inside. It ain't his idea not to get away. He just begins to feel it ain't no point in fightin. He becomes a prisoner to the human's demand. But with Willow, I ain't never made it impossible for her to get away. I might 'ave made it not real easy because of the way I wrapped the rope around the post, but it weren't impossible. It was her choice, her decision to keep pullin or not.

"Tyin a horse solid is black and white to a horse. He had betta give up or kill himself tryin. There ain't no grey area that asks him to search and use his brain and make up his own mind what's best for him. Anythin that is black or white or doesn't give a horse choices is bad trainin. Nosebands that keep a horse's mouth shut or hobbles to get him to stand still or tie downs to make him keep his neck down are all takin away a horse's choice.

TRAINING AND CHOICES

"When ya take away his choices, he ain't gonna change how he feels. He might get real submissive and real polite, but he ain't gonna feel okay inside. If ya don't get a horse to feel betta inside, ya ain't got anythin worth spit. Ya got no more to offer a horse than them doggers at the market."

So I told my client that you can get a horse to change how he feels by offering him choices and encouraging him to search through those choices. It's not always easy because some horses have been trained to be so shut down that they don't know how to search. Saddler stores are full to the ceiling with equipment designed to take choices away from a horse. For most people this is not a problem because they don't see the difference in the outcome. But then I believe if we do this we have no right to claim our horses love to work and that we love our horses – they are just words without meaning.

WHY IS IT SO?

Walt and Amos always kept pretty much to themselves. At the riding school where I worked as a kid most people gave them a wide berth. It's not that Walt and Amos were rude, mean or unfriendly; it's just that they went about their business and left others to do the same. They were old and didn't have much to say. Small talk was definitely not their strength. Apart from me they didn't have many friends at the riding school. Nevertheless, other boarders gossiped about them all the time. People could see that they had a way around horses, and it was not the way that any of the other horse folk went about handling and riding. So while they thought the two old men were strange and had some very different ideas about horses to their own, people were wary but intrigued about the twin brothers.

In the early days of my career as a stable and tack cleaner, groom and general lackey, I noticed that people would ask each other why Walt or Amos would do things the way they do. Somebody might see Amos use a flag on a horse and ask another person why he did it and what was it for. Inevitably, the answer was not known and Amos would be dismissed as a crank. I remember one instant when I overheard a small group of people talking about how Walt or Amos never rugged their horses – not even in winter! After much discussion it was concluded they probably couldn't afford to buy their horses a rug, so the poor horses went without. It never cross the minds of those people that Walt and Amos would have a good reason why leaving their horses bare was better for the horses than rugging.

Over time, as some of the longer term boarders became more use to seeing Walt and Amos around the place and familiarities (if not friendships) were formed I began to notice than some folk began to ask Walt and Amos about some of the stuff they did. It began with the occasional observation followed by a question.

"Hi Walt, that's an interesting set of reins ya got there. Gee they're heavy. Why are they so heavy?"

"Well, I like them split reins 'cause if ya ridin in the bush and a rein gets hung up on a bush, ya can let the rein go and pick it up again when ya through the bush. It means the horse don't get jabbed in the mouth 'cause ya rein got stuck on somethin. But the weight keeps the rein on the neck where I left it even if the horse is goin fast over rough country. It also makes for a smoother feel in the horse's mouth – no need for big movement 'cause with a weight like this the horse can feel a fly land on the leather. It also gives the horse a better feel if I need to neck rein him."

Inevitable, the person would walk away with a clearer understanding of why Walt used that type of rein. People's interest in the habits of the old fellows came in dribs and drabs. Usually it came about because somebody was having a problem and didn't know where to turn. In their desperation they might ask Walt or Amos.

"Amos, I was wonderin if you could look at Cammy. I rode her this morning and she feels like she is stepping over hot coals."

"Well, it looks to me that she is steppin toe first instead of heel first. Probably got some heel pain 'cause ya let the toe grow too long and the heels too tall. See how the heels all contractin and the frog looks shrivelled up? Yup I think she's pretty sore. Ya oughta talk to ya farrier about getting this fixed before any serious damage get's done."

The longer I knew Walt and Amos the more respect I developed for their minds. That may seem strange considering they never attended high school and they were never seen with a book in their hands. But what was to became obvious to me and every body else who took the time to talk to them about horses is that they were never stumped for a reason as to why they did the things they did. Never once did I hear them say they do it this way or use such-and-such gear or feed a certain type of grain or trim a horse's feet in a specific manner just because they had seen somebody else do it that way or they were taught to do it that way. Everything they did around horses had been deliberately thought out and chosen because it made the most sense to the brothers. It didn't matter if it was as simple a thing as tying a knot to the more complex a concept of breaking a horse in. I have never known people who were as careful as Walt and Amos about the things they did with horses.

I was very lucky to know Walt and Amos for many years. When I was very young and first met the old men, most of what they did was different from what I had seen before. I looked at them as oddities. I was extremely curious about their way around horses. I knew they were out on left field all by themselves and considered them nothing more than interesting. I certainly didn't want to be like them or do things like them. I wanted to ride, train, handle and treat horses the way everybody else did. So my curiosity about Walt and Amos was expressed by questions as to why they did things. I was always asking them why. Why did they mouth a horse without a bit? Why did they use a breast collar on their saddle? Why did they use their outside leg the way they did? Why did they do so much groundwork? Why did they teach their horses tricks?

As I grew older and my knowledge and understanding about horses grew with me I began to see the logic and the results behind why the old men rode, trained and handled horses the way they did. Some of these things became incorporated into my own approach to the horses. I wasn't always aware of it, but I later realized that changes were taking place in the way that I thought about the things I did with horses. It wasn't so much that I just started to take on board the ideas of Walt and Amos, but that I started to question the stuff I was already doing. Were there good reasons for it and if not what was a better approach? I began to question myself. It was hard at first because change is always difficult. But as I learned to question my own ideas I started to question the things others said and did. Even Walt and Amos! One of the more interesting aspects of my new enquiring approach to was that my questions sometimes changed from "why do you do it this way", to "why don't you do it this way?" In fact, Walt and Amos made a point of letting me know this change in my thinking. I would ask "why don't you rug your horses, why don't you use the outside rein in a turn, why don't you use a martingale, why don't you use leg in a rein-back, etc?"

The funny thing is that today I see some parallels between my experience with Walt and Amos and the reaction I get from some horse folk. People who know nothing about me often dismiss me as having some odd practices around horses. Recently, somebody was talking about me and said that they didn't understand why anyone would use a flag – it just seemed a stupid thing to do and didn't make sense. But they never asked me about the flag and why I use it. In their understanding and in the world of what they do with a horse, the flag had no place. They didn't use one, their friends did not use one and their teachers did not use one, so what was the point?

Then the second group of people are those that generally make up my clients. They like what I do and the results that I get with a horse, but they don't quite get it, yet they want to understand. From these people I get the "why do you..." type of questions.

The last group of people are those that have been around me for a long time and have a good understanding of why I do the things that I do. But they are still grappling with why others don't have the same ideas. These people ask the "why don't I ...." type of questions.

In order to be able to answer the questions of all these people I try very hard to make sure that I have a good reason and understanding of everything that I do. At a recent clinic that I gave, somebody mentioned to me that they had never been to any trainer who had thought so much about everything they do. I was very pleased with this compliment because it is important to me that I understand and can justify to myself the approach I take in my work. I never want to just accept the word or teaching of somebody else. I may try things that seemed like a good idea, but then either dismiss them or incorporate them or modify them depending on the responses of the horses.

It's hard to think for ourselves when we are unsure – especially when everyone around us is telling us what to do even if they themselves don't necessarily understand why. But I see so much poor horsemanship because the person accepted the word of their instructor or a clinician or a friend or read it in a book. Question everything. Ask why you do the things you do. Make sure you have a good understanding and even more important make sure the horse is better for it. Then when you are comfortable with the answers you can start to ask why don't you do it the way other people do it.

www.ingramcontent.com/pod-product-compliance
Lightning Source LLC
Chambersburg PA
CBHW032046150426
43194CB00006B/440